Reuse and Recycling — Reverse Logistics Opportunities

COUNCIL OF LOGISTICS MANAGEMENT

2803 Butterfield Road, Oak Brook, IL 60521-1156 • (708) 574-0985 • Fax # (708) 574-0989

Reuse and Recycling — Reverse Logistics Opportunities

Transmode Consultants

Ronald Kopicki, Principal

ICF Incorporated

Michael J. Berg, Vice President
Leslie Legg, Senior Associate

Contributing Authors -- ICF Incorporated

Vijetha Dasappa, Senior Associate
Cara Maggioni, Analyst

COUNCIL OF LOGISTICS MANAGEMENT

2803 Butterfield Road, Oak Brook, IL 60521-1156 • (708) 574-0985 • Fax # (708) 574-0989

ACKNOWLEDGEMENTS

Identifying the opportunities for logistics professionals provided by reuse and recycling programs across a broad section of American industry is a formidable task. We could not have begun this task without the assistance and guidance of many individuals and organizations who offered their time, information, and informed opinions. Foremost, we would like to thank the Steering Committee of the Council of Logistics Management, which conscientiously guided our efforts throughout the project. We would also like to acknowledge the valuable contributions of Kenneth E. Novak, W.W. Grainger, Inc., who chaired the Steering Committee, and the other Committee members, Daniel J. Kemna, Waste Management of North America, Inc., James R. Stock, University of South Florida, David R. Hartman, The Coca Cola Company, and Elaine M. Winter, Council of Logistics Management.

Developing the case study materials presented throughout this book required an investment of time and resources by the companies we investigated. We would like to acknowledge the value of their contributions and that of their employees. In particular, we would like to thank the following individuals and the companies they serve: *Aveda*, Thomas Balf, Environmental Affairs Director, and Patrick Faust, Distribution Center Manager; *Bristol-Myers Squibb Pharmaceutical Group*, Kathleen C. Doyle, Senior Director, Logistics; *Chep USA*, Gary F. Garkowski, Vice President, Marketing; *E.I. du Pont de Nemours and Company, Inc.*, Frank N. Aronhalt, Director, Environmental Affairs and Polymer Recycling, and Edward J. Falkowski, Director, Imaging

Environmental Services; *The Home Depot*, Mark Eisen, Manager
of Environmental Marketing, James Ardell, Northeast Regional
Distribution Manager, and Peter E. Cleaveland, Vice President of
Traffic and Distribution; *McDonald's Corporation*, Robert L.
Langert, Director of Environmental Affairs, Lynn Heinlein
McRecycle USA Coordinator, Ray Croaston, and Aristides Smith
(formerly with TRIACE, a McDonald's service company); *Mindis
Recycling*, L. Keith Rinzler, Vice President of Development;
National Electrical Manufacturers Association, Lisa D. Silverstone,
Section Staff Executive; *Nike*, Henry Chriss, Director,
Environmental Action Department, Lisa Garner, Paula M. Harris,
and Leta Winston, Environmental Action Department, and
Dan Wright, Administrative Services Department; *North American
High Value Products*, Edward H. Dobie, Area Vice President,
Customized Logistics Services; *Owens-Brockway*, James Hiltner,
Recycling Manager; *Portable Rechargeable Battery Association*,
Norm England, President; *Procter & Gamble*, Thomas Rattray,
Associate Director, Corporate Packaging Development; *RE-
SOURCE AMERICA INC.*, Wayne Williams, Vice President of
Technology; *Scientific Certification Systems*, Chet Chaffee,
Director, Environmental Marketing and Linda G. Brown, Vice
President, Communication; *Sears, Roebuck & Co.*, Keith Tice,
National Director of Packaging and Labeling; *Waste Management,
Inc.*, Paul E. Aeschleman, Environmental Marketing Specialist,
and Larry Burris, President, Waste Management Tri-Cities; *Xerox*,
James S. McDonald, Manager of Product Logistics; and *Zytec*,
Robert Mallett, Value Analysis Manager.

In addition, we would like to thank three individuals who
provided us with their independent perspective on developments
in reverse logistics as well as with valuable insights gained
through their own extensive experience in the field. Specifically,

we would like to thank Cliff Sayre, for his early and formative contribution to this work; Omar Keith Helferich of Michigan State University, for the well informed dialogue and advice that he offered throughout our study; and Thomas Speh of Miami University, for his review of the book in its final draft form. All these individuals added value to our efforts and provided perspectives from which we would not otherwise have benefited.

Finally, we acknowledge the valuable contribution and thank our colleagues at Transmode Consultants and ICF Incorporated who provided review, advice, and assistance in researching and writing this book. In particular, we would like to thank Paul Roberts of Transmode and Chris Bailey, Michael Lanz, and Scott Walsten of ICF Incorporated for their valued contributions. In addition, we are grateful to Margo D. Brown for her able assistance with the layout and typing of this book.

Without the help of all these people our efforts would have fallen short of the final result. We sincerely thank them all.

TABLE OF CONTENTS

CHAPTER 4. INBOUND LOGISTICS: RECYCLING
            SUPPLY CHAINS

CHAPTER 5. WASTE REDUCTION IN THE FORWARD
            DISTRIBUTION SYSTEM

CHAPTER 6. DESIGNING REVERSE DISTRIBUTION
            SYSTEMS FOR REUSE AND RECYCLING

CHAPTER 7. THIRD-PARTY SERVICES

PREFACE

This study invites logisticians to get involved in designing and implementing reuse and recycling programs. Reuse and recycling represent the leading edge of corporate environmental activism during a period when successful management of environmental issues is becoming vital to corporate success. Although environmental programs often have a regulatory or public relations focus, the economics of reuse and recycling depend substantially on efficient materials handling and transportation. These programs can clearly benefit from greater involvement by logisticians.

This study identifies four elements of reuse and recycling programs that could benefit most from the expertise of logistics professionals:

(1) Adapting inbound supply chains to using materials recovered from new municipal waste recycling programs;

(2) Creating reuse and recycling programs for packaging waste in forward distribution systems;

(3) Taking back products from customers for reuse and recycling; and

(4) Creating new third-party services to facilitate the recovery of in-plant wastes and used products.

Information on each of these topics is presented in a general "how to" format that identifies the current impediments to efficiency and suggests approaches for resolving them. Designing efficient reuse and recycling programs is challenging. Logisticians who resolve the difficulties and implement successful programs can create a competitive advantage for their companies.

EXECUTIVE SUMMARY

Increased social concern about solid waste management is transforming the relationship between environment and business and creating new roles for logistics professionals. The majority of the public no longer believes that environmental protection and economic growth are incompatible objectives.[1] Instead, the private sector in cooperation with government is expected to find new ways of making environmental protection profitable for individual firms as well as the society as a whole. Programs to reduce and recycle waste and to market products with less environmental impact are at the forefront of corporate environmental strategies. The success of these programs often depends on finding creative solutions to logistics problems, which gives corporate logistics professionals new opportunities to contribute to a growing field.

This book is designed as a managerial guide to planning and implementing waste reduction programs. It kindles awareness of the emerging issues and options in non-hazardous waste reduction for logistics professionals. It also describes how these issues affect the supply chain, and reviews examples of practical actions that a firm can take to be proactive in reuse, recycling, and source reduction. Other types of reverse logistics practices, such as waste disposal and hazardous waste management, are generally outside the scope of this book.

To begin the book, this chapter briefly describes:

♦ Key concepts involved in waste reduction programs;

- ◆ Broad trends in waste management practices and the pressures and potential value of corporate waste reduction initiatives;

- ◆ Corporate opportunities for logisticians created by increased social concerns about waste management; and

- ◆ The purpose and organization of this book.

1.1 Key Concepts

Recycling and reuse programs are encompassed within the concept of "reverse logistics." As defined in the Council of Logistics Management's 1991 white paper entitled "Reverse Logistics,"[2] reverse logistics encompasses the logistics management skills and activities involved in reducing, managing, and disposing of wastes. It includes reverse distribution, which is the process by which a company collects its used, damaged, or outdated products or packaging from end-users. This study focuses on the reuse and recycling aspects of reverse logistics and, to a lesser extent, on source reduction. Each of these three areas -- recycling, reuse, and source reduction -- is encompassed within the broader term of waste reduction.

Most companies' involvement with <u>recycling</u> is limited to generating recyclable materials and consuming products with recycled content. Recycling, however, is actually a four-stage process that involves:

(1) Collecting recyclable materials from waste generators;

Key Terms

Municipal Solid Waste *(MSW) is post-consumer non-hazardous solid waste generated by households, commercial establishments, institutions, and light industry. MSW generally excludes construction and demolition debris, most scrap metal, and non-hazardous materials discarded from industrial operations or derived from manufacturing processes.*

Recycling *is the process by which materials otherwise destined for disposal are collected, processed, and remanufactured into new products. Composting organic materials is a form of recycling.*

Reuse *is the use of a product or component part in its same form for the same use without remanufacturing. Reuse may be considered as a form of source reduction.*

Reverse Distribution *is the process by which a company collects its used, damaged, or outdated products and/or packaging from end-users. Reverse distribution is a subset of reverse logistics.*

Reverse Logistics *is a broad term referring to the logistics management skills and activities involved in reducing, managing, and disposing of hazardous or non-hazardous waste from packaging and products. It includes reverse distribution, as defined above, which causes goods and information to flow in the opposite direction of normal logistics activities. This book focuses narrowly on the non-hazardous waste reduction activities of the reverse logistics process.*

Source Reduction *entails reducing the amount and/or toxicity of material destined to enter the waste stream.*

Waste Reduction *is a broad term that encompasses recycling, reuse, and source reduction.*

(See Chapter 12 Glossary for additional definitions.)

(2) Processing recyclables to create raw materials, which are called secondary, as opposed to virgin, materials;

(3) Using these secondary materials to manufacture new products; and

(4) Returning the products to commerce.

Composting is a specialized form of recycling. Composting, the controlled biological decomposition of organic solid waste under aerobic conditions, produces mulch or soil amendments. While yard waste composting is common in the United States, communities and private firms are also experimenting with composting food waste and other organic materials.

Private waste services firms usually collect, process, and market recyclables generated by other companies and households. The firms in this existing infrastructure vary from large international waste collection and management firms, such as Waste Management Incorporated and Browning Ferris Incorporated, to small firms specializing in particular types of wastes (e.g., paper, automobile parts, or glass) and/or particular stages in collecting and processing recyclables. The logistics of recycling becomes an issue for companies outside the traditional waste management industry when these companies assume responsibility for recycling their in-house wastes, reclaiming their products or packaging from consumers, or purchasing secondary materials as manufacturing inputs.

Reusing products such as pallets involves a process similar to recycling, except that instead of processing the products to create raw materials, the products are refurbished or repaired and used again in their original form. Reuse requires creating reverse distribution channels so that used goods are returned to manufacturers or remanufacturers. <u>Source reduction</u> involves reducing the amount and/or toxicity of material consumed or wastes generated (e.g., lightweighting packaging). Reuse may be considered as a type of source reduction.

These waste reduction activities affect all areas of the company, including finance, marketing, research and development, manufacturing, and public relations. They directly and often significantly affect logistics management. Moreover, logistical skills are often critical to their success, as secondary materials are collected and transported to manufacturing facilities; packaging from the distribution chain is recycled, reused, and reduced; and products are taken back from end-users.

As waste reduction programs expand and mature in response to public and regulatory pressures and market opportunities, the demand for logistics expertise will multiply. The relatively fluid nature of the organizational structure surrounding these programs will often enable logistics staff to easily join emerging organizations that demand their skills.

1.2 Changing Waste Management Practices and Pressures

Unlike global warming or depletion of the ozone layer, waste management is not a new environmental problem. At the end of the 19th century, local officials were looking for solutions to the lack of suitable sites for garbage dumps and to the complaints of residents in proximity to the dumps. But this age-old problem of what to do with our garbage is transforming the adversarial relationship between environmental goals and business objectives into a cooperative partnership.

The garbage problem resurfaced as a prominent topic of national concern in the mid-1980s, when Mobro, the Long Island Garbage Scow, roamed the Atlantic seaboard looking for a landfill to take its load of trash. This news story helped publicize the dwindling numbers of landfills in the United States. Between 1978 and 1988, more than 70 percent of operating municipal landfills closed as they reached capacity or failed to meet increasingly stringent environmental standards.[3]

Less publicized was the fact the Mobro began its voyage because of a contract dispute between the transfer station that had accepted the trash and the designated disposal facility. After being rejected by six states and three countries, the scow finally dumped its load at a Brooklyn incinerator and the resulting ash was deposited in a Long Island landfill. In parallel, the fact that the landfills that replaced closed facilities, though fewer in number, are much larger in size was not widely known, primarily because national data are not available to document changes in net capacity. These examples illustrate that the shortage of landfill space may be less serious than it appears to be. Nevertheless the landfill shortage remains a potent symbol of solid waste concern.

Over the last 20 years, several factors have combined to bring solid waste disposal to the forefront of environmental concerns:

♦ Stricter regulations for municipal waste incinerators and landfills caused many local facilities to close.

♦ High construction costs for new facilities, combined with public opposition to the development of replacement facilities, triggered a disposal "crisis" in many communities.

♦ Conventional refuse collection and disposal patterns were displaced in favor of regional agreements which required more planning and negotiation between municipalities and waste management service providers.

Looking for the cause of waste disposal problems, the public fixated on symbols of the modern convenience lifestyle, such as fast food packaging and diapers, as causes of the landfill problem, despite the fact that these items use only a small fraction of landfill capacity. Instead, the fastest growing categories of discards over the last two decades were as follows:

♦ Appliances (up 74 percent), which parallels the increased number of households and common household appliances in the United States;

♦ Furniture (up 80 percent), which largely reflects the increased number of households;

♦ Paper products (up 24 to 211 percent depending on the grade), which largely reflects the shift to a service-based economy from manufacturing.[4]

While the use of packaging increased dramatically during the first part of the century, packaging's 29 percent share of municipal solid waste discards in 1990 is slightly lower than its share of discards in 1960, due to the use of lighter weight materials and increased recycling.[5]

Recycling, and to a more modest extent, source reduction, became the public's solutions to waste management problems. Recycling allayed broader concerns regarding wasteful consumption patterns and satisfied the urge to conserve resources. As people realized that recycling ultimately involved returning products to commerce and that source reduction was largely in the hands of manufacturers, businesses were drawn into the situation as potential partners, not just as targets of product bans or other regulatory mandates.

If disposal problems are not as severe as the public seemingly believes, why should firms establish waste reduction initiatives? Corporate reuse and recycling programs are often motivated by regulatory, employee, and public pressures, as described below.

♦ **Minimizing current and potential future regulatory compliance costs.** Commercial waste recycling is already mandatory in some states. Businesses that do not comply are subject to fines and other civil and, in some cases, criminal sanctions. Products whose packaging does not meet waste reduction standards can lose access to domestic and international markets. Regulatory compliance achieved by minimizing wastes may create competitive cost advantages and avoid enactment of more burdensome legislation, such as product bans. In addition, proactive waste reduction programs may facilitate enactment of legislation that creates a competitive advantage for the firm.

♦ **Improving employee morale.** Many corporate waste reduction programs are initiated by environmentally concerned employees. Firms with poor environmental records may face staff recruitment and retention difficulties.

♦ **Improving public image.** As described in Chapter 2, environmental concerns are affecting the purchasing habits of many consumers. Positive press coverage of a firm's waste reduction programs can be more effective and credible in communicating with the public than expensive advertising campaigns.

Instead of merely responding to these pressures, forward-looking corporations seek to create value and competitive advantages by developing superior capabilities in reuse and recycling. Reuse and recycling programs have the potential to produce tangible financial benefits for a firm by:

♦ **Reducing procurement, manufacturing, and waste disposal costs.** Reusing products and otherwise reducing materials usage can lower costs. Recycled materials are often less expensive than virgin materials. In addition, reducing the volume of waste discarded through recycling may lower waste management costs and create new revenue sources through sales of recyclable material. Overall, source reduction activities generally have the greatest potential cost savings potential.

♦ **Meeting customer demands.** Companies are increasingly requiring their suppliers to meet environmental standards (e.g., minimum recycled content, reduced packaging). In addition, the demands of retailers for maximum selling space and lower disposal costs can be met by new reduced or recyclable packaging designs.

♦ **Creating new market opportunities.** Market opportunities may be created in both products and services. "Green" products that meet other customer criteria may have a competitive edge. Recycling and reuse is also creating opportunities in the transportation services industry, as many firms are relying on third parties to collect, consolidate, and transport recyclable and reusable materials.

Companies can maximize the benefits or value of reuse and recycling programs by involving logistics personnel in program design and management. Logistical skills are often crucial because recycling and reuse are logistics intensive.

1.3 Opportunities for Logisticians

Responsibilities for waste management are increasingly shared by consumers, retailers, distributors, manufacturers, and third parties, in addition to the traditional providers of waste services: local governments, scrap dealers, and other private waste collection and management companies. Businesses are being asked or required to reduce and recycle their own wastes. Manufacturers are being required to assume more responsibility for recycling, reusing, or disposing of their products and packaging. Consumers are demanding that manufacturers design products with less environmental impact, less packaging, and more recycled content. To implement these programs, manufacturers are taking actions including, but not limited to:

♦ Modifying inbound supply chains to purchase recyclable materials and products with recycled content;

♦ Establishing recycling and reuse programs for their own wastes; and

♦ Developing reverse distribution capabilities to take back products and packaging from end-users.

These pressures are blurring the distinctions between the responsibilities of logistics personnel and environmental affairs departments within many companies. In some instances, new departments have been created. As companies advance from environmental strategies that react to new regulatory mandates to environmental strategies designed to maximize the value of the firm's recycling and reuse capabilities, the logistics department or staff is likely to gain new responsibilities for managing waste reduction within their own departments and facilitating waste reduction activities for the entire firm.

New environmental strategies will often require modifying existing supply chains and delivery systems. Furthermore, corporate environmental strategies may also build on the skills of logistics professionals to enter new markets. For example, firms may build on a core competency in logistics to become third-party providers of transportation, handling, storage, and regulatory compliance services for recycling and reuse programs.

Logistics staff can also make vital contributions to other aspects of corporate or industry-wide environmental strategies. As reduced or reusable packaging designs are developed, for example, logistics personnel are in the best position to evaluate the impacts on distribution systems and to work with carriers, public warehouses, and other distribution channel members to implement such changes. The product flows orientation of logistics professionals is also uniquely suited to helping evaluate the environmental impacts of potential new "green products" as they move through different stages of their life-cycle, from raw materials procurement to distribution and use of finished goods.

Chief executive officers committed to waste reduction programs often cite the attitudes of middle managers within their firms as one of the biggest obstacles to program implementation.[6] Logistics personnel have the opportunity to differentiate themselves by advocating environmental initiatives and finding creative ways of implementing them to reduce costs and increase revenues. Conversely, logistics managers who do not actively participate in developing environmental programs may find themselves responsible for addressing difficulties created by poor planning decisions, such as disputing liability for damaged products with carriers due to inappropriately "reduced" packaging or processing recyclables at warehouses that were not designed to handle them.

1.4 Purpose and Organization

The purpose of this book is to provide logistics managers with
a practical guide and reference handbook for planning and
implementing corporate reuse and recycling programs. This book
incorporates the findings of a series of detailed interviews with 17
firms that are acknowledged leaders in recycling, reuse, and
related aspects of reverse logistics. The companies chosen for
case study interviews typically had annual revenues exceeding
$50 million and represented a diverse range of business activities
(e.g., manufacturing, retailing, and services). It is organized as
follows:

♦ Chapter 2 summarizes evolving public attitudes and
laws regarding reuse and recycling.

♦ Chapter 3 describes the phases in the development of
recycling and reuse programs.

♦ Chapters 4 through 7 analyze and present examples of
four aspects of waste reduction programs from a
logistics perspective:

(1) Tailoring inbound supply chains for recyclables
and recycled content products;

(2) Establishing recycling, reuse, and source
reduction programs to minimize packaging
waste in the forward distribution system;

Reuse and Recycling

      (3) Developing reverse distribution capabilities to take back products and packaging from end-users; and

      (4) Using third-party recycling, reuse, and take-back services.

♦ Chapters 8 and 9 present detailed case studies of innovative programs in two leading-edge firms, DuPont and The Home Depot.

♦ The book ends with the conclusions, a list of information sources, and a glossary in Chapters 10 through 12 respectively.

Endnotes

1. *Green Consumerism: Commitment Remains Strong Despite Economic Pessimism*, Cambridge Reports/Research International, Cambridge, MA, October 1992.

2. James R. Stock, *Reverse Logistics*, Council of Logistics Management, Oak Brook, IL, October 1992.

3. *Garbage Then and Now*, National Solid Wastes Management Association, Washington, DC, April 1990.

4. Gary Tanhauser, "Packaging in the '90s," *Garbage*, December/January 1993, page 27.

5. *Characterization of Municipal Solid Waste in the United States: 1992 Update*, prepared for the U.S. EPA, Office of Solid Waste by Franklin Associates, July 1992, pages 2-34 to 2-42.

6. Managers may oppose these programs because they often believe that the costs of environmental programs will not be able to be passed on to consumers. Pieter Winsemius and Ulrich Guntram, "Responding to the Environmental Challenge," *Business Horizons*, March/April 1992, page 19.

WASTE REDUCTION TRENDS

2

2.1 Introduction

What is driving the environmental movement? Will public support for recycling fade? Is green marketing just another fad? How can a company respond to consumer demands for more environmentally friendly products with the ever-changing standards for what is best for the environment? This chapter attempts to answer these questions as part of a background briefing on the evolution of public attitudes toward the environment and solid waste reduction laws.

The chapter is organized into four additional sections:

♦ Section 2.2 profiles changes in the environmental movement between Earth Day 1970 and Earth Day 1990, illustrating the growth of concern for environmental issues.

♦ Section 2.3 examines public attitudes toward the environment and recycling in the United States and abroad.

♦ These attitudes are reflected in current trends in United States' solid waste reduction legislation, discussed in Section 2.4.

♦ The chapter concludes with a brief summary of the trends in solid waste legislation in other economically developed nations.

2.2 Earth Day 1970 Versus 1990

On April 22, 1990, the nation celebrated the 20th anniversary of Earth Day. The media had been closely following the preparation for the event for months; the January 1989 cover issue of *Time Magazine* was devoted to the "Year of the Planet." Over the past two decades, the U.S. Environmental Protection Agency (EPA) was created and major laws were enacted by Congress to promote resource conservation, improve waste management practices, and control industrial emissions.

The environmental movement had come a long way from the unexpectedly successful grassroots teach-in organized by Gaylord Nelson, a Wisconsin Senator, in 1970. While the first Earth Day organizing committee had a budget of only $150,000, the event was celebrated by 20 million people across the country.[1] Conservation of energy and other natural resources was a major theme. Students buried automobiles and protested air and water pollution and roadside litter. Corporate participation in the event was minimal. At the local level, environmental enthusiasm often translated into recycling programs organized primarily by non-profit groups. Between 1968 and 1974, the number of communities with any newspaper recycling program grew from two to 134. Many programs, however, were later terminated due to poor markets for recyclable materials.[2]

While the first Earth Day is frequently seen as a purely spontaneous outpouring of public concern for the environment, it is more accurately defined as a celebration of attitudes about the environment that had been evolving since World War II. Samuel Hays, an environmental historian, links protective attitudes toward the environment to the general quest for improved quality of life made possible by rising public affluence and increased leisure time after the war. For the first time, large sectors of the population could escape congested cities for homes in the suburbs and vacations in national parks. This led to greater public appreciation of the environment for its aesthetic qualities and amenities.[3] At the same time, the shift in employment from agriculture and natural resource extraction industries to service industries meant that fewer people had a direct stake in using the environment as an industrial resource.

Over the two decades following the first Earth Day, the public desire to protect the environment evolved into a belief that the survival of nature was threatened by human activities and that human health was threatened by environmental pollution. A series of real and perceived environmental disasters, such as the Love Canal hazardous waste site, the chemical gas leak in Bhopal, India, the wandering garbage barge, Mobro, and the Exxon Valdez oil spill, overwhelmed more modest stories about the success of the environmental laws enacted in the 1970s in reducing air and water pollution. In addition, global warming and the destruction of the rain forests emerged as new threats that seemed to jeopardize the survival of the entire planet. In an era when control of infectious diseases reduced mortality from "natural causes," people were also becoming more concerned about the ability of environmental pollution to cause long-term illnesses such as cancer.

Reflecting the growth of the environmental movement, the Earth Day 1990 celebration was a much larger affair than its predecessor 20 years earlier. Two organizations were formed to promote the Earth Day anniversary. The larger group, run by the 1970 national Earth Day coordinator Dennis Hayes, had a budget of $3 million.[4] Earth Day 1990 was dedicated to the new concept of "sustainable development," an idea popularized in the late 1980s. Sustainable development promotes economic activities that will ensure protection of the planet for future generations. The concept changes the conflict between environmental goals and economic development into a cooperative search for solutions.

Media coverage of Earth Day 1990 activities included sweeping stories of global problems threatening the health of the planet, specific stories of what consumers and businesses could do to save the earth, and profiles of new corporate environmental initiatives. Many consumer recommendations and new business programs involved waste reduction. Consumers were urged to recycle their wastes and to change their purchasing habits to buy recycled-content, recyclable, or reusable products with minimal packaging. Companies announced new green packaging and products and started their own waste recycling programs.

Companies actively sought to be involved in Earth Day 1990. Although Earth Day activities were primarily at the local level, large corporations were directly involved in sponsoring, planning, and hosting activities for their employees and the general public. Only 10 companies, however, were allowed to serve as "official" Earth Day sponsors or board members because the organization turned down offers from any companies in the timber, chemical, and petroleum industries. Ultimately, Earth Day prompted many corporations to begin examining their own activities to find ways of making a positive contribution to environmental protection.

2.3 Public Perspectives on Waste Disposal and the Environment

Questions naturally arose as to whether Earth Day 1990 and the activities it inspired were simply a passing fad sparked by the period of economic growth in the 1980s. Research from Cambridge Research/Reports International, a company that has been conducting polls of public attitudes toward the environment since the 1970s, found that public concern about environmental issues accelerated sharply in the late 1980s and has generally stabilized at high levels or continued to grow, despite the recession in the early 1990s.[5] In addition, surveys of the business community support the notion that environmental concerns will not fade away; most corporate executives believe that waste reduction regulations and requirements worldwide will become more stringent in the future.

The remainder of this section discusses the following aspects of public opinions on the environment:

♦ The relative importance of environmental concerns;
♦ The continued strength of these concerns;
♦ Solid waste as an environmental concern;
♦ Recycling as a solution to solid waste problems;
♦ The advent of green consumerism; and
♦ International views on the environment.

Environmentalism and the Economy

Most Americans do not rank the environment as one of the most important issues facing the country, yet they strongly believe in the need for environmental protection. Economic, national security, and social issues, such as race relations, drugs, and the homeless, have historically taken precedence over environmental concerns. In 1992, only eight percent of the population identified the environment as one of the two most important issues facing the United States.[6] Similarly, in Gallup polls from 1935 through 1990, the majority of respondents named an environmental issue, energy concerns, only twice as among the nation's most important problems. Even then, energy concerns may have been related primarily to rising oil and gas prices that helped spur calls for energy conservation.[7]

Despite these rankings, people appear willing to make economic sacrifices for environmental protection. In July 1992, Cambridge Reports/Research International surveyed 1,250 adults in the United States about green consumerism and the economy and found the following:[8]

♦ Almost 70 percent of the population say they are willing to pay higher prices (about $40 per month on average) to protect the environment and 56 percent say they are willing to pay five percent more in income taxes.

♦ More than ever, Americans believe environmental protection is compatible with economic growth.

♦ The majority of Americans feel that an investment in the environment would create more jobs than it would eliminate.

Public support for the environment begins to falter only when the public is given a direct choice between increased protection and higher levels of unemployment. Then, only 29 percent would continue to favor more protection as opposed to job security.[9]

Continued Strength of Environmental Concerns

Public support for the environment remained strong after Earth Day 1990, despite the recession of the early 1990s. In fact, the vast majority of Americans now consider themselves environmentalists, and participation in environmental organizations has continued to increase. For example:[10]

♦ In 1992, more than 70 percent of Americans identified themselves as environmentalists.

♦ The portion of people who reported donating to or being active in an environmental group increased from 15 percent in 1987 to 42 percent in 1992, the highest level ever.

♦ The number of people who reported changing their daily behavior to protect the environment also reached a historic high of 80 percent in 1992.

This willingness to act on environmental issues seems to be motivated largely by increasing concerns about deteriorating environmental quality. More than 40 percent of people believe that the overall quality of the air they breathe is worse than it was five years ago, and 37 percent think that the quality of their drinking water is worse now than five years ago.[11] Only a quarter of the population thinks that air quality and drinking water quality have improved.

Solid Waste as an Environmental Concern

When asked to rank environmental issues, people place solid waste disposal below air pollution and water pollution, but above such issues as hazardous waste and global warming. Views on the severity of the solid waste disposal problem are almost evenly divided: 48 percent view it as very to somewhat serious, and 45 percent regard it as not too serious or not serious at all.[13]   In

> **Business Leaders Expect to Reorganize to Meet Environmental Goals**[12]
>
> *Most industry environmental programs have been organized to ensure regulatory compliance. A 1991 McKinsey survey of 400 corporate executives worldwide found that this mindset is changing. While only 13 percent of the executives had begun to integrate environmental concerns into corporate strategy and even fewer (nine percent) had begun to realize new environmental marketing opportunities, many executives felt a need to reorganize to meet future environmental goals. More than 60 percent felt that industry must re-think its entire concept of industrial processes to adapt to an increasingly environment-conscious world.*

contrast, a U.S. Environmental Protection Agency panel recently ranked solid waste disposal sites as a low health risk relative to indoor air pollution and radon, pesticides, and drinking water contamination.[14]

The public readily identifies what it believes is the most troublesome material in solid waste. Seventy-seven percent of those surveyed identified plastic as playing a large to moderate role in the solid waste disposal problem. Local officials and the waste management industry tend to cite public opposition to waste disposal facilities -- the "not in my backyard" or NIMBY factor -- yet the public did not view this as a significant cause of the waste disposal problem.[15]

Recycling: The Public's Solution

The American public is virtually unanimous in identifying a solution to the solid waste problem: recycling. Ninety-five percent of those polled feel that a major national commitment to recycling would substantially reduce the amount of solid waste disposed. Forty-one percent of these respondents feel that a major commitment could reduce waste disposal from 21 to 50 percent. Forty-five percent feel that waste could be reduced by more than 50 percent. The number of people in this latter category more than doubled between July 1988 and October 1992.[16] To reach these levels would require substantial changes in current waste management practices; in 1990 only 17 percent of the nation's municipal waste was recycled or composted. People also report voluntary and community mandated changes in their daily behavior, such as recycling cans, bottles, or paper.[17,18]

New markets need to be developed for the increasing amounts of recovered material. The majority of people believe that both industry and government are not doing enough to solve waste disposal problems.[19] Forty-eight percent agree that industry should be primarily responsible for this task, while 33 percent believe that government should have primary responsibility.

The Advent of Green Consumerism

In addition to recycling, people are changing their daily behavior by acting on environmental concerns at the supermarket. Close to 70 percent of respondents agree with the statement that buying and using environmentally friendly products is the most important thing they can do to preserve the environment.[21] The degree to which consumers act on these opinions, particularly when environmentally friendly products are more expensive, is still uncertain.

> ### Registering Concerns at Checkout Counters[20]
>
> *Actions people report taking to protect the environment:*
>
> ♦ *Pay a premium for environmentally friendly products (81%);*
>
> ♦ *Regularly buy products with recycled content (53%);*
>
> ♦ *Frequently avoid products with excessive or environmentally harmful packaging (37%); and*
>
> ♦ *Frequently avoid products made by companies they perceive as harming the environment (29%).*

Successfully marketing products as environmentally friendly can be a challenge. The Cambridge Green Consumerism Survey found that consumers are skeptical about the accuracy of environmental labeling claims. Only 55 percent believe that a product labeled as environmentally friendly is actually better for the environment. (Regulations governing environmental labeling are discussed in Section 2.4.)

Concern About the Environment Is Even Stronger Abroad

To coincide with the 1992 United Nations Conference on the Environment in Rio de Janeiro, Brazil, an affiliate of Gallup Polls commissioned a study of environmental opinions in 22 nations representing all levels of economic development around the world.[22] The poll found that environmental protection was a major international issue. Approximately half of the nations surveyed ranked environmental issues among their top three concerns.

Majorities in most nations believed that environmental pollution was affecting their health at the time and would pose a threat to their children and grandchildren. Air and water pollution were regarded as the most serious problems. Most respondents implicated industry and industrial processes as the cause for this pollution. Improved technology, product bans, and more stringent regulation of businesses were believed to offer the best solutions. People in the United States, in contrast, were more likely to blame environmental problems on individuals.

Respondents in almost all of the surveyed nations gave priority to environmental protection, even at the risk of slowing economic growth. A majority in 16 of the 22 nations expressed a willingness to pay more for environmental protection. The United States ranked in the bottom half of high-income countries in its willingness to pay. Finally, in 16 countries, over half of the survey respondents reported avoiding products perceived as harmful to the environment. People in Western Europe, Scandinavia, Chile, and Canada are more likely than people in the United States to avoid environmentally harmful products.

2.4 Trends in Solid Waste Reduction Legislation

Recent solid waste legislation has been crafted to address public perceptions of a landfill capacity crisis. These laws are causing the infrastructure for collecting and processing recyclables in solid waste to expand rapidly.

In the United States, state governments have taken the lead on solid waste reduction by enacting more than 400 solid waste and recycling laws from January 1988 through December 1991.[23] In contrast, federal recycling requirements are currently limited to collection standards for federal agencies and a procurement program for the purchase of recycled products by federal agencies. More extensive federal standards for recycling are expected when Congress amends the Resource Conservation and Recovery Act (RCRA).

The first state recycling laws focused on the supply-side of recycling by developing collection programs for recyclable materials, primarily from single family homes. Then, as the materials collected exceeded the demand in some areas and caused prices to drop throughout the country, states enacted demand-side laws to stimulate markets through such measures as minimum content requirements, enhanced recycled product procurement programs, and tax, grant, and loan programs.

Both supply- and demand-side requirements affect logistics within an organization. Compliance with these laws may require establishing new distribution routes to take back products and packaging, new warehouse layouts to store reusable or recyclable materials, and third-party agreements with secondary material processors and manufacturers. The trend toward demand-side laws and source reduction programs is likely to increase the responsibilities of logistics professionals because the regulations tend to target manufacturers rather than local governments.

This section describes the following types of state legislative trends in the United States:

♦ Collection and disposal requirements, specifically mandatory container deposits, mandatory recycling laws, and disposal bans;

♦ Market development laws regarding product take-back requirements, minimum recycled content requirements, environmental labeling, financial incentives, and recycled product procurement; and

♦ Source reduction laws, including model legislation and product bans.

This section also describes model and proposed legislation at the state and federal levels.

Collection and Disposal Requirements

Mandatory Container Deposits. Although mandatory container deposits (bottle bills) were originally enacted to reduce roadside litter, they became the first state requirements for recycling. Oregon enacted the first bottle bill in 1972. Eight other states followed suit by 1983. In 1987, California enacted a modified version of the bottle bill, which requires collection centers to be sited in convenient locations -- usually grocery store parking lots. Numerous other attempts have been made to enact state bottle bills and a federal bottle bill, but they have all been defeated.

Bottle bills have created a reverse distribution infrastructure for soft drink and beer containers. In bottle bill states, a deposit, usually between 1 to 10 cents, is placed on beer and soft drink containers to induce consumers to return the containers to retailers. Retailers sort containers by brand and return them to distributors, who send them back to manufacturers. Although bottle bills are commonly associated with refillable containers, most returned containers are not refilled, but are manufactured into new containers.

Bottle deposit laws have achieved very high rates of return (e.g., 70 to 90 percent) and have helped to reduce roadside litter. Nevertheless, these laws are strongly opposed by the beverage industry, which finds refillable containers generally more expensive to manufacture and transport than "one-way" containers. Instead, the soft drink industry and many policy analysts favor multi-material curbside collection programs and buy-back centers over bottle bills.

Mandatory Recycling Laws. As shown in the figure below, most states have adopted mandatory recycling laws. These laws take many forms, including recycling goals for state or local governments, curbside collection requirements, commercial recycling requirements, and more general mandates for local governments to establish recycling programs. Most were enacted during the mid to late 1980s and many states have yet to develop enforcement mechanisms. Primarily as a result of these mandates, however, the number of curbside collection programs for recycled materials increased by almost 500 percent, from just

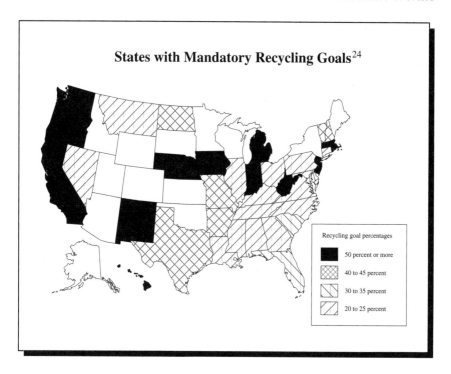

States with Mandatory Recycling Goals[24]

Recycling goal percentages

- 50 percent or more
- 40 to 45 percent
- 30 to 35 percent
- 20 to 25 percent

over 1,000 programs in 1988 to 5,404 programs in 1992.[25] Seven states (Connecticut, Maine, New Jersey, New York, Pennsylvania, Rhode Island, and Wisconsin) plus the District of Columbia now require businesses to separate recyclables from their trash.[26] Local governments trying to meet state mandates may also require businesses to recycle.

Disposal Bans. Thirty-seven states have banned certain products or materials from landfills and incinerators.[27] Most of those states ban lead-acid batteries (e.g., from automobiles). Other prohibited wastes include leaves, grass clippings, other yard waste, tires, used oil, small batteries, and appliances.

Reuse and Recycling

Wisconsin and Rhode Island have extended bans to traditional recyclables such as paper and various forms of packaging. In Wisconsin, the disposal of most paper and packaging materials is banned unless communities are certified by the State as having effective recycling programs. In Rhode Island, designated recyclables are banned from commercial waste disposal.

Disposal bans are intended to foster recycling, but as originally enacted, the laws typically do not require manufacturers or retailers to collect or use the recovered materials. Instead, waste generators and haulers bear the compliance burden of keeping the materials out of trash containers and disposal facilities. Disposal bans coupled with higher waste collection costs are motivating retailers to request reusable or recyclable packaging from manufacturers and distributors.

Market Development Laws

Product "Take-Back" Requirements.[28] These laws extend the mandatory beverage container deposit concept to other products, such as appliances, batteries, tires, used oil, and telephone books. Unlike the original bottle bills, most recent take-back laws were enacted to save landfill space or reduce pollution from disposal of these items. Many have been enacted to secure markets for products subject to disposal bans. Not all of the take-back requirements involve deposits and refunds, but they do impose the responsibility for recycling products on the manufacturers, distributors, and/or retailers. Specific take-back requirements have been established for the following products:

♦ **Appliances.** Retailers and wholesalers in Illinois, for example, are required to take back the white goods they sell.

♦ **Batteries.** Model legislation from the Battery Council establishes a deposit on new lead-acid battery sales that is refunded when customers return old batteries to retailers. At least nine states have deposit systems. Another 15 states just require retailers and wholesalers to accept old batteries. In addition,

  ▸ Vermont, Minnesota, Rhode Island, and New Jersey require manufacturers of nickel cadmium batteries to set up recycling programs with goals of recovering 90 percent of these batteries.

  ▸ Connecticut and Maryland have take-back requirements for button batteries.

♦ **Ozone-depleting substances.** Under the mandate of the federal Clean Air Act Amendments of 1990, persons servicing motor vehicle air conditioners must use certified recycling equipment to recover chlorofluorocarbons and other ozone-depleting refrigerants. Similar recycling requirements apply to ozone-depleting substances used in industrial process refrigeration and other appliances.

♦ **Packaging.** In Florida, manufacturers are not required to recycle, but if at least 50 percent of specified packaging materials are not recycled by mid

1993, a one cent retail tax will be imposed per container. The tax rate may rise to two cents by 1995.

♦ **Tires and used oil.** Taxes on the sale of new tires and used oil are more common than deposits on these goods. The revenues are usually placed in a state recycling fund and distributed to local governments or private companies to fund recycling projects. Retailers selling these items are required to accept them for recycling and to post signs about the recycling program.

♦ **Telephone books.** Connecticut and Rhode Island require telephone book distributors to make their product recyclable, holding them responsible for collecting and recycling the used books. Distributors, however, may be able to pay a fee to the state or local government to have the books included in municipal collection programs.

Minimum Recycled Content Requirements. Minimum content laws require manufacturers to include specified amounts of recycled content in certain products or packaging. As shown in the figure below, minimum content standards for newsprint are most common, but a few states have targeted other products, such as plastic bags, plastic containers, glass containers, and telephone books. Recycled content mandates single out products that collectors and processors of recycled materials have had difficulty marketing. Thus, these laws often result in closed loop recycling systems (e.g., old telephone books are used to make new telephone books).

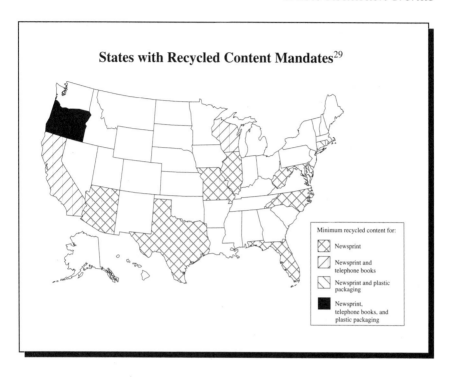

States with Recycled Content Mandates[29]

Minimum recycled content for:

Newsprint

Newsprint and telephone books

Newsprint and plastic packaging

Newsprint, telephone books, and plastic packaging

More minimum content standards may be forthcoming because they appear to produce the desired results, as exemplified by newspaper recycling. In the late 1980s, newsprint markets were flooded by the dramatic increase in old newspapers from curbside recycling programs. As a result, many communities suddenly had to pay to have their newspaper recycled. Newsprint producers and publishers had initially been reluctant to use more old newsprint, citing concerns about quality, unstable supplies, and a recent expansion in virgin newsprint production capacity. After Connecticut and California enacted minimum recycled content laws for newsprint publishers in 1989, the industry position changed. Publishers generally negotiated voluntary agreements with state officials to avoid legislated minimum content mandates. As of late 1992, 27 mills in North America had the capacity to de-ink newsprint for recycling, up from just nine mills in 1989, and another 12 deinking mills were in planning stages.[30] Some industry analysts are predicting that by the mid 1990s deinking capacity may outstrip the demand.

Environmental Labeling. To respond to consumer preferences for environmentally friendly products, more manufacturers have been advertising the environmental benefits of their products, and some retailers have begun labeling systems for green products on store shelves. To date, no consensus exists on how environmental claims should be evaluated. Currently, at least 13 states, two private organizations, Green Cross and Green Seal, and two federal agencies, EPA and the Federal Trade Commission (FTC), are creating their own definitions and logos for recycled, reusable, reduced, and otherwise environmentally friendly products or packaging.

During the summer of 1992, the FTC issued guidelines for environmental claims to help reduce existing confusion. (Although states are encouraged to use the FTC guidelines as a model for their own laws, they are not required to adopt the guidelines.) The FTC discourages broad claims such as "green" or "environmentally friendly" and provides guidance on using terms such as recyclable, reusable, reduced, refillable, compostable, degradable, recycled content, and ozone safe. To claim that a product is recyclable, for example, the entire product must be able to be incorporated into manufacturing processes for new products and the majority of customers should have access to recycling facilities. If access is not widely available, the FTC advises including a disclaimer. Companies that do not comply are notified by the FTC. If a company continues to make false claims, it may be prosecuted for false and misleading advertising.

The Recycling Advisory Council (RAC), a joint National Recycling Coalition and U.S. Environmental Protection Agency venture, has developed more detailed guidelines for labeling recycled content in paper products. The RAC standards apply to all paper and paperboard products and differentiate between post-consumer waste and paper recovered during the manufacturing and printing process. RAC also provides a formula for calculating percentages of recycled content. These standards are expected to be incorporated into federal guidelines for procuring products with recycled content.

Financial Incentives. Approximately half of all states have encouraged businesses to recycle by establishing financial incentives, such as tax credits, grants, and low interest loans. Incentives typically apply to investments in equipment that process recyclables into raw materials. At least 20 states provide tax credits to companies for purchasing recycling equipment or using recycled materials in their manufacturing process.[31] The magnitude of these incentives is often small relative to the large sums needed to invest in manufacturing equipment for secondary materials, such as deinking lines for newsprint that can cost several hundred million dollars. Some states have also been willing to provide special tax exemptions to entice companies to site major manufacturing facilities using secondary materials in their state.

Recycled Product Procurement. Thirty-five states and the federal government have price preferences or set-aside programs for products with recycled content. The state programs usually apply to paper, but are being expanded to include other materials. Federal procurement guidelines are in place for paper and paper products, re-refined oil, building insulation, cement and concrete containing fly ash, and retread tires. Procurement laws have the potential to substantially stimulate the development of recycling markets; state and local government purchases account for 12 to 13 percent of the U.S. gross domestic product.

Source Reduction Laws

Although source reduction is commonly viewed as environmentally preferable to recycling, states have been slow to enact source reduction legislation. Reducing the amount and toxicity of material in products inherently involves changing manufacturing processes, which states have been reluctant to regulate. In addition, source reduction is a much more ambiguous concept than recycling, raising issues such as the feasibility of measuring waste not produced. Nevertheless, a few states include source reduction as a method for achieving state waste reduction goals. Otherwise, the only major source reduction laws that have been enacted involve reducing the use of toxic materials in packaging, which are discussed below. Bans on the sale of products perceived to be "wasteful" are also discussed in this section, but these laws generally result in materials substitution without real reductions in waste or toxicity.

CONEG Model Toxins Reduction Laws. The Coalition of Northeastern Governors (CONEG) has developed model legislation limiting the amount of lead, mercury, cadmium, and hexavalent chromium in packaging. According to the Coalition, these toxic reduction laws have been adopted by 16 states and were under consideration in three others as of July 1993. The model law exempts packaging made from recycled materials and certain packaging essential for product protection.

Product Bans. While many bans have been proposed on the sale of certain products thought to cause major solid waste disposal problems (e.g., plastic packaging and diapers), relatively few bans have been enacted. A few states have banned disposable products, such as coffee cups, in state offices and several municipalities have banned polystyrene. The local bans have not taken effect, however, due to court decisions or industry agreements to fund recycling programs instead. Product bans seem to be losing popularity unless they are linked to other requirements, such as the CONEG toxins reduction law. The bans do not necessarily reduce waste, since many of the items would simply be replaced by products that take up equal or more landfill space.

Pending and Proposed U.S. Waste Reduction Legislation

In recent years, more than 2,000 bills related to solid waste disposal and recycling have been introduced annually in state legislatures and Congress. This section discusses model packaging legislation that has been introduced at the state and federal levels, and other major bills that have been introduced as part of the reauthorization process for the federal Resource Conservation and Recovery Act (RCRA). These proposals reflect the trend towards increasing manufacturer responsibility for the recycling, reuse, and source reduction of products and packaging.

Model State Packaging Reduction Legislation. At the state level, CONEG and the Massachusetts Public Interest Research Groups (MASSPIRG) have each introduced model legislation to reduce packaging waste. Proposals based on these models have also been introduced at the federal level.

The CONEG model legislation would require a 15 percent reduction in packages or packaging components entering the waste stream by 1996 compared to 1988 levels. The legislation would give packaging manufacturers two options for compliance:

(1) **Company-wide approach.** Starting from a base date of January 1, 1988, at the company level, a packager could use a variety of reduction methods (i.e., source reduction, reuse, recyclability, or recycled content in any combination) to achieve the standard.

(2) **Specific package approach.** Alternatively, a packager could be required to ensure that each package or packaging component meets one or more specified criteria by January 1, 1996:

- ♦ Source reduced by 10 percent from the base date;

- ♦ Reusable or refillable five or more times;

- ♦ Contain at least 25 percent recycled post-consumer materials; or

- ♦ Recycled at a rate of at least 25 percent by weight.

The model legislation contains exemptions for certain medical and food products, businesses with 15 or fewer full time employees, flexible packaging components of 10 millimeters or less in thickness, and situations where compliance would impose a hardship on the citizens of the state.

The Massachusetts chapter of the U.S. Public Interest Research Group (PIRG) has a slightly different proposal. Under this model, packaging would have to meet one of five recycling standards, all aimed at reducing waste from packaging and creating a market for the materials collected by local recycling programs. Under this proposal, packaging must be:

◆ Reusable 5 or more times;

◆ Made of at least 25 percent recycled materials by 1996, 35 percent by 1999, and 50 percent by 2002;

◆ Made of materials that are actually being recycled at a rate of 25 percent (35 percent by 1999 and 50 percent by 2002);

◆ Reduced by 25 percent every five years; or

◆ Recycled itself at a 50 percent rate.

Neither the CONEG or PIRG models have been fully adopted at the state or federal levels. California and Oregon, however, have enacted laws that are similar to these models that apply only to rigid plastic containers. Under the PIRG and the CONEG model legislation, firms that violate requirements would be subject to monetary sanctions.

Reuse and Recycling

RCRA Reauthorization. More than 175 bills relating to RCRA reauthorization were introduced in the U.S. Congress in 1992. While none of these bills was enacted, RCRA reauthorization is likely to be an environmental priority during the Clinton administration. Based on the bills introduced in 1992, the main features of the reauthorization debate are outlined briefly below.

♦ The primary focus of future reauthorization is likely to be on solid waste issues, including solid waste from both households and businesses.

♦ Many proposals will mirror existing state laws, including recycling and source reduction goals, minimum content standards, packaging regulations (based on the CONEG and PIRG models), and management standards for selected "problem" wastes, such as used oil, batteries, or tires. Thus, federal action could establish uniform minimum standards throughout the nation.

♦ The bills could also allow states or local governments to restrict interstate transport of solid wastes. Although these restrictions are motivated by a desire to restrict shipments of waste from the Northeast to the Midwest, they also affect the hundreds of shipments of waste between adjacent states and deter interstate shipments of garbage for processing to recover recyclables.

In addition, economic incentives to address solid waste problems are also likely to receive a lot of attention, such as taxes on virgin materials.

2.5 International Waste Reduction Laws and Trends

Recent legislation in Western Europe may portend the future direction of recycling in the United States. New curbside collection programs and materials recovery facilities in the United States have generally been financed by local governments and subsidized by state grants.[32] In contrast, the new European packaging laws impose the primary responsibility on industry. Selected examples of recent legislation in other nations are discussed below.[33]

German Model of Manufacturer, Distributor, and Retailer Responsibility

The German Waste and Packaging Law enacted in April 1991 is expected to shape recycling policy for the rest of the continent and is being closely watched by policy-makers in the United States as well. The ordinance holds manufacturers, distributors, and retailers responsible for recycling packaging waste. Germany is also considering similar take-back requirements for household appliances and automobiles.

Under the Waste and Packaging Law, manufacturers were to begin collecting and recycling transport (or tertiary) packaging as of December 1991. By April 1992, distributors and retailers were required to collect secondary packaging. And by January 1993, a system was to be established to recycle primary packaging which consumers could leave at retail stores. Companies importing goods to Germany would have to arrange for the collection and recycling of their packages.

Rather than relying on the option of retail collection of packaging, over 400 companies, including large multinationals, have formed a new private waste company, the Duales System Deutschland (DSD), which provides curbside collection of designated recyclables from households. Sixty percent of most packaging materials must be recycled by January 1993 and at least 80 percent must be recycled by 1995. Packaging that does not meet the goals will be subject to large deposits. Packages included in the DSD system are marked with a green dot. Companies must pay a fee (up to 12 cents per package as of early 1993) for the symbol based on the expense of processing the material.

The ultimate impact and cost of this initiative remains to be determined, but the recycling rates are widely regarded as extremely ambitious. For example, the paper and paperboard recycling rate was just 40 percent in 1987, and the glass recycling rate was 53 percent in 1989. Little information is currently available on the effectiveness of the new system. News reports have documented shortages in processing capacity and flooded recycling markets in other countries as a result of an influx of German recyclables.

Scandinavian Refillable Requirements

Scandinavian countries have focused their waste reduction efforts on beverage containers. In Denmark, beer and carbonated drinks, including imports, must be packaged in refillable containers and are subject to a deposit. Aluminum cans are banned. Both Finland and Norway tax non-refillable beverage containers. Sweden imposes a tax on all cans, which is redeemable for aluminum, and has banned non-refillable polyethylene terephalate (PET) plastic containers.

Great Britain's Approach

England's approach to recycling most closely resembles the U.S. system. England has more landfill space than most other countries and is said to be less environmentally active than other western European countries. England must comply with a United Kingdom goal of recycling 50 percent of the recyclable component of household waste by the year 2000. English municipalities are currently experimenting with curbside recycling programs. Under the U.K. system, any disposal cost savings from recycling are to be transferred through a credit system to waste collection and recycling companies. Eventually, the responsibility for recycling may be transferred to an organization sponsored by the packaging industry.

Netherlands' Source Reduction Efforts

The Dutch government has detailed long-term plans for merging economic development with environmental protection. The plans involve developing standards for green product and process design through voluntary agreements with industry. Companies have already agreed to reduce the total amount and weight of packaging and to discontinue using any materials found by an independent authority to be environmentally unfriendly. In turn, the government program is investing in clean technology; the technology program had a budget of $90 million in 1990.

European Community Recycling Standards

To resolve discrepancies in legislation between member countries, the European Community proposed a "New Approach Standard" for reuse and recycling in July 1992. The standard would replace current packaging rules in member countries. If adopted by EC council members, the directive will require countries to recover 90 percent of all materials in the waste stream (up from an estimated average 18 percent recycling rate at present) and recycle 60 percent of all the material in the packaging within 10 years of enactment. Incineration with energy recovery and composting would both count towards the 90 percent goal, but incineration does not count toward the 60 percent target. Packaging would need to be labeled as reusable or recyclable or contain recycled content. The proposal also includes limits for lead, cadmium, mercury, and hexavalent chromium in packaging that start at 600 ppm and decline to 100 ppm after five years from the date of enactment.

Japanese Mandates

Although Japan is often depicted as a world leader in recycling, the country did not enact a mandatory recycling law until 1991. Shortages of both land and natural resources drove municipal waste recycling in Japan to levels between 26 and 39 percent in the mid 1980s.[34] The new law sets a recycling goal of 60 percent by the mid 1990s for most materials, including packaging, paper, and batteries. It also establishes product redesign standards for both packaging and durable goods. The recycling law reflects Japan's belief that environmentally sound products and technology will provide major new markets for

Japanese companies. Significantly, the law is sponsored by the Ministry of International Trade and Industry.

Existing International Labeling Laws

Canada, Germany, Japan, and several Nordic countries have established environmental labeling programs. The European Community has also designed an eco-label, but has yet to set a date to begin implementation. The labeling programs either rank products based on a single attribute, such as energy use, or assess the total environmental impact of a product from production through disposal. Not surprisingly, the single-attribute programs are able to certify more products, but the labels may not be as meaningful as labels developed using a more comprehensive framework.

Key Findings

✓ *Public support for environmental protection continues to grow and increasingly influences consumer behavior.*

✓ *Industry will continue to respond to public concerns through environmental marketing.*

✓ *Future legislation will likely increase private sector, particularly manufacturer, responsibility for product recycling, reuse, or disposal.*

✓ *Legislation adopted in many states includes not only collection and disposal requirements, but also product and packaging take-back requirements, minimum recycled content standards, and environmental labeling standards.*

Endnotes

1. Adam Shell, "Earth Day Spawns Corporate Feeding Frenzy," *Public Relations Journal*, February 1990, page 9.

2. Louis Blumberg, Robert Gottlieb, *War on Waste, Can America Win Its Battle With Garbage?*, Island Press, Washington DC, 1989, page 200.

3. Samuel P. Hays, *Beauty, Health, and Permanence, Environmental Politics in the United States, 1955-1985*, Cambridge University Press, Cambridge, England, 1987, pages 22-24.

4. Adam Shell, "Earth Day Spawns Corporate Feeding Frenzy," *Public Relations Journal*, February 1990.

5. *Green Consumerism: Commitment Remains Strong Despite Economic Pessimism*, Cambridge Reports/Research International, Cambridge, MA, October 1992.

6. *Omni Survey Results*, Cambridge Reports/Research International, Cambridge, MA, October 9-21, 1992.

7. "Despite Dissatisfaction with Way Things Are Going, Most Americans Remain Positive About Personal Lives and the Future," Gallup Poll News Service, July 25, 1990.

8. *Green Consumerism: Commitment Remains Strong Despite Economic Pessimism*, Cambridge Reports/Research International.

9. Ibid, page 16.

10. Ibid, pages 7, 8, and 18.

11. *Public Priorities for Environmental Protection and Economic Growth*, Cambridge Reports/Research International, Cambridge, MA, December 1992. (September 1992 survey results.)

12. Pieter Winsemius and Ulrich Guntram, "Responding to the Environmental Challenge," *Business Horizons*, March/April 1992.

13. *Omni Survey Results*, Cambridge Reports/Research International.

14. *Comparing Risks and Setting Environmental Priorities, Overview of Three Regional Projects*, U.S. EPA, Office of Policy Planning and Evaluation, August 1989, page X.

15. *Omni Survey Results*, Cambridge Reports/Research International.

16. Ibid.

17. *Green Consumerism: Commitment Remains Strong Despite Economic Pessimism*, Cambridge Reports/Research International, page 21.

18. Graham Hueber, "Americans Report High Levels of Environmental Concern, Activity," The Gallup Poll News Service, April 20, 1991.

19. *Omni Survey Results*, Cambridge Reports/Research International.

20. *Green Consumerism: Commitment Remains Strong Despite Economic Pessimism*, Cambridge Reports/Research International.

21. Ibid, page 21.

22. Riley Dunlap, George Gallup, Jr., and Alex Gallup, *The Health of the Planet Survey*, George H. Gallup International Institute, Princeton, NJ, July 1992.

23. *Special Report: Recycling in the States (1988, 1989, 1990 editions)*, National Solid Wastes Management Association, Washington, DC; *State Recycling Laws Update, Year-end Edition*, Raymond Communications, Riverdale, MD, February 1992. All of the information in the following section is derived from these reports unless otherwise noted.

24. Chaz Miller, Recycling in the States: 1992 Update, *Waste Age*, March 1993, page 28.

25. Robert Steutville and Nora Goldstein, "1993 Nationwide Survey: The State of Garbage in America," *Biocycle*, May 1993.

26. *Special Report: Recycling in the States 1990 Review*, National Solid Wastes Management Association, Washington, DC, September 1991, page 7.

27. Ibid, pages 31-32.

28. Jim Glenn, "1992 Nationwide Survey: The State of Garbage in America," *Biocycle*, April 1992; Raymond Communications, *State Recycling Laws Update, Year-end Edition*, Riverdale, MD, February 1992.

---

29. Chaz Miller, Recycling in the States: 1992 Update, page 30.

30. Phone conversation with Paul Boyle, American Newspaper Publishers Association, Reston, VA, December 1992.

31. Chaz Miller, "Recycling in the States: 1992 Update," page 32.

32. The private waste industry that runs many municipal recycling programs may be indirectly financing them by taking a lower rate of return on their municipal contracts for recycling compared to refuse collection. Some of the state grant money is also derived from industry sources through selected product taxes and surcharges on tipping fees.

33. Primary sources for this section include *Green Products by Design, Choices for a Cleaner Environment*, Office of Technology Assessment, Washington, DC, October 1992; and Frances Cairncress, "How Europe's Companies Reposition to Recycle," *Harvard Business Review*, March/April 1992, pages 34-35.

34. *Facing America's Trash: What Next for Municipal Solid Waste?*, U.S. Office of Technology Assessment, Washington, DC, October 1989, page 136.

PHASES OF REUSE AND RECYCLING PROGRAM DEVELOPMENT

3

3.1 Introduction

Many companies are responding to pro-environmental public attitudes and the resulting flurry of waste reduction legislation by establishing reuse and recycling programs. These programs vary in their purpose, scope, and impact on corporate operations. In general, ambitious programs initiated in advance of legislation have greater consequences for logistics personnel and a greater need for logistics expertise than those initiated in reaction to legislation.

Interviews with 17 companies and an extensive literature review revealed that reuse and recycling programs often follow a three-phase pattern of development:

- Phase 1: Reactive,
- Phase 2: Proactive, and
- Phase 3: Value-Seeking.[1]

These phases represent increasing levels of corporate commitment to waste reduction and related environmental concerns. This model of corporate responses to solid waste issues is comparable to other models of corporate environmental awareness, which are typically derived from corporate experiences with laws governing hazardous waste and air and water emissions.[2]

From a purely environmental standpoint, firms should move steadily towards Phase 3. Because the market does not always place a high value on environmental objectives, however, firms may not find it worthwhile or possible to reach Phase 3. Further, corporate recycling and reuse programs do not necessarily fit neatly into any one phase; at any given time, they may include activities typical of more than one phase.

The three phases of this model also mirror corporate approaches to implementing total quality management programs. Both programs involve progressing from adopting a few specific practices to embracing a new corporate philosophy or culture:

♦ Phase 1 reuse and recycling programs correspond to improving quality control procedures.

♦ Phase 2 program activities are similar to drafting a quality policy and implementing some new quality management practices, such as just-in-time delivery.

♦ Phase 3 program activities resemble quality programs that have become a primary focus of operations and lead to empowering employees, seeking continuous improvement, and exceeding customer expectations.

This chapter is organized as follows:

♦ Sections 3.2 to 3.4 describe the characteristics of each phase of reuse and recycling program development, including program goals, typical activities, organization, and resources. These characteristics are summarized in the following table. For brevity, the chapter describes only the new goals and activities associated with each phase.

Phase	Goals	Activities	Organization	Resources
Reactive	Comply with existing laws Fulfill individual environmental commitments Achieve cost savings	Recycle corrugated cardboard, office paper, and beverage containers Procure products with recycled content Label products that are recyclable, contain recycled material, or have other environmental benefits	Usually an ad-hoc and decentralized organization Responsibility falls on individual who initiates program or, if program reacts to laws, government affairs or environmental compliance office Use of third parties to collect waste for recycling	Minimal Costs may increase for recycled paper and containers to collect and store recyclable materials Compliance costs vary by location
Proactive	Preempt new environmental laws by voluntarily starting programs Develop competitive advantage through more efficient compliance Sell products that satisfy customers' environmental concerns	Prepare a corporate environmental policy statement and define environmental performance goals Perform environmental audit Purchase more recycled materials Recycle or reuse pallets, plastics, defective products, and process wastes Design green products and services Assume responsibility for product reuse and recycling through industry coalitions and reverse distribution programs	Commitment of CEO and other top managers One or two new program manager positions Managers may have any background, from public relations to merchandising to packaging Broad communication of program objectives to all employees Interdepartmental committees may establish priorities	Modest Possibly seek to avoid high costs by entering into joint ventures or industry coalitions

The Three Phases of Corporate Waste Reduction Programs (continued)

Phase	Goals	Activities	Organization	Resources
Value-Seeking	Integrate environmental activities into a business strategy Operate the firm to reduce its impact on the environment	Use environmental life-cycle analysis to evaluate products and packaging Design products for disassembly and recycling or reuse Create competitive advantage in reverse distribution programs Ask suppliers to commit to waste reduction goals Use third parties in reverse supply chains Develop internal incentives and enforcement mechanisms Critically review and reassess existing processes, products, and services	CEO and other top managers establish strong environmental commitment Interdepartmental teams help set policies and identify areas for improvement Waste reduction managers coordinate and implement policies throughout firm Each department encouraged to contribute ideas and take initiative	Difficult to calculate because the program becomes integral to all of company's operations Capital exposure often limited by partnerships with third parties

♦ Section 3.5 analyzes the implications of reuse and recycling program development for logistics personnel.

♦ Section 3.6 presents a case study of the evolution of McDonald's reuse and recycling program.

3.2 Phase 1: Reactive Approach

Reactive programs are usually a response to external pressures on a company's products or practices, although occasionally they arise from pressure by employees. Reactive programs are narrow in scope. They are designed to avoid disrupting traditional business practices. In Phase 1, few companies perceive that a significant strategic value can be derived from their recycling and reuse programs.

Program Goals

Companies design Phase 1 programs to address specific issues or concerns. Reactive programs will thus have specific goals, such as:

- **Comply with existing state and local laws.** As discussed in the previous chapter, waste reduction laws may require companies to separate their waste for recycling, use recycled content in products, eliminate toxic additives in packaging, or take back used products for recycling or disposal.

- **Fulfill individual environmental commitments.** Many recycling programs are started by individual employees who are concerned about the environment.

At Nike, for example, employee efforts to divert defective shoes collected at a distribution center from landfills led to the design of a shoe containing materials recycled from the defective shoes.

- **Capture cost savings.** Most companies do not initiate recycling programs to save money. Cost savings or the ability to break even, however, may determine whether non-mandated activities are undertaken. For example, the disposal costs avoided by recycling may spur firms to recover materials that would otherwise be disposed of.

Typical Activities

Although recycling and reuse programs and other environmental concerns are not a part of the business strategy of firms with Phase 1 programs, these firms frequently:

- **Recycle corrugated cardboard, office paper, and beverage containers.** The company usually administers the collection system within its buildings and contracts with material brokers or waste management companies for subsequent transportation, processing, and marketing.

- **Procure products with recycled content.** Such printer and copier paper can be ordered from existing suppliers. Companies involved in government contracting may be required to use paper products with recycled content. Using such materials may require changes in printing and photocopying equipment.

- **Label products that are recyclable, contain recycled content, or have other environmental benefits.** While firms may readily modify their product labels, activities that involve changing the product, service, or distribution system are undertaken only if required by law.

Organization

Phase 1 programs are usually organized on an ad hoc and decentralized basis. Individual employees or a single department within a company implementing Phase 1 programs may not be able to affect change throughout the firm. Furthermore, Phase 1 program activities are often supplementary to regular job responsibilities.

The locus of responsibility within the firm also varies. If a program results from individual initiative, responsibility for managing the program will usually fall on those who initiated the program, regardless of their regular duties. If the program is mandated by law, however, responsibility for managing it will likely fall on the government affairs department or an environmental compliance office. Maintenance staff are frequently involved with implementing office recycling programs. Large institutions may hire a recycling coordinator to implement internal recycling programs and manage contracts with third parties.

Resources

Expenditures for voluntary reuse and recycling programs are minimal. Companies may spend slightly more to purchase some recycled products, such as copy paper, or new containers needed to collect and store recyclable materials. Expenditures to comply with take-back laws or recycled content mandates vary according to product type and the current state of remanufacturing technology for that material. These costs can be significant if investments in new equipment are required.

3.3 Phase 2: Proactive Approach

Proactive programs to reduce, reuse, and recycle solid waste signal a new wave of corporate environmental action. Companies adopting this approach believe that developing extensive waste recycling programs and greener products in advance of potential statutory mandates is in their best interests. For example, companies with progressive green product or waste reduction practices may be invited to participate in roundtable discussions and working groups with government agencies that help shape future environmental rules. By bringing experience with a voluntary program to the negotiating table, these companies will possess substantive knowledge about program feasibility and costs and are more likely to have their concerns considered. Future regulations are likely to be modeled on the programs or ideas of participants in the policy-making process, giving these firms an advantage over their competitors.

To date, the firms most likely to establish proactive programs are those that deal directly with individual consumers. These companies include retailers and consumer product companies whose product lines may be threatened by potential product packaging bans. In addition, companies such as 3M and DuPont that realized savings from hazardous waste reduction and benefitted from better public relations by taking a pro-environmental stance are often willing to invest in proactive ventures for non-hazardous waste.

A proactive program, especially one involving green marketing, may not succeed immediately. Some U.S. firms have aggressively responded to public

---

Benefits of Being Proactive

"Environmental protection and competitiveness are not mutually exclusive. When environmental regulations apply to everyone, the company that meets them most effectively has a cost advantage over those that do not. Environmental performance is a new business variable that will be with us from now on. Companies that drag their heels and view it as a burden will chase numbers from year to year and just get by. Companies that see environmental performance as an opportunity to innovate and leap ahead of the competition will gain. Once a company has decided to inculcate an awareness of environmental protection into all its activities and direct its efforts in a manner that gains competitive advantage, then efforts to address specific issues of policy will be more focused and will have more credibility."

Dr. Kaahr, Vice President of Environmental Policy, DuPont

---

demand for environmentally friendly products by developing new products and changing their advertising strategies to promote the products' environmental attributes. Green marketing is currently a relatively high risk strategy because of the lack of both national priorities for environmental protection and agreement on the definitions of key environmental attributes, such as recyclable or compostable. In addition, public perceptions of correct environmental choices change rapidly as new information proves old assumptions incorrect or uncovers previously unconsidered environmental impacts. For example, a once widely accepted theory on the degradability of waste in landfills was recently demonstrated to be incorrect.

When the landfill capacity "crisis" became national news in the late 1980s, degradable products, especially plastics, were accepted as a means of dramatically extending the lifespan of landfills. The findings from a series of landfill excavations conducted by a University of Arizona garbage archeologist, William Rathje, debunked these conceptions. His studies revealed that landfills function more like dry tombs than compost piles. Digging in landfills across the country, Rathje uncovered carrots intact after 10 years burial, and newspapers still legible after 30 years.[3] Companies that promoted degradable plastic bags and other products were discredited and threatened with lawsuits for false advertising.

Program Goals

Phase 2 waste reduction programs tend to be more sophisticated than Phase 1 programs and will often be part of broader environmental programs. They will therefore have broader, less specific goals that require more thought and planning to implement. Common goals include the following:

- **Preempt potential waste reduction laws by starting programs voluntarily.** The newspaper industry, for example, has negotiated voluntary recycled content agreements with 11 states in an effort to deter the enactment of recycled content laws. Similarly, the plastics industry has created aggressive recycling and public education programs to deter regulatory mandates, such as bans on the disposal of plastic waste and recycled content mandates.

- **Develop a competitive advantage through more efficient regulatory compliance.** A company that finds an efficient way of meeting new regulations or that already operates in a manner consistent with new environmental regulations will have a strategic advantage over its competitors.

- **Market new green products and services designed to satisfy customers with environmental concerns.** For example, Procter & Gamble (which has a Phase 3 program) introduced a refill package for its Downy Fabric Softener. Within a year of its introduction, the refill package represented 40 percent of all sales of Downy Fabric Softener. This waste reducing product clearly helped satisfy some of P&G's customers' environmental concerns.[4]

Typical Activities

Proactive programs have internal and external components. Internal activities, geared to better management of waste within the company, are necessary to maintain the credibility of external efforts, such as promoting green products. In this phase, a company may:

- **Prepare a corporate environmental policy statement.** This document codifies the company's approach to environmental issues and establishes guidelines for incorporating environmental concerns into business decision-making. When participants from throughout the firm are responsible for drafting the statement, the process can be almost as valuable as the statement itself for raising environmental awareness within the firm. Some companies have modeled their statements after

> **The CERES Principles**
>
> *In 1989, the Coalition of Environmental Responsible Economies (CERES), an organization of environmental groups, socially conscious investors, and pension fund trustees, drafted a statement of environmental principles for corporations. Companies that sign the CERES principles agree to follow a number of practices, including ameliorating adverse environmental impacts created by their operations, striving to reduce environmental impacts, institutionalizing responsibility for environmental affairs within top management, and publishing an annual environmental audit.*
>
> *Initial signatories were primarily small companies that had few environmental liabilities. In 1993, CERES revised the principles to address corporate concerns that agreeing to the principles could increase corporate liability. In February 1993, Sun Company, an oil and gas firm, became the first Fortune 500 corporation to sign.*

the CERES Principles (originally the Valdez Principles.)

- **Define environmental performance goals that reflect the policy statement.** Typical waste reduction goals include numerical targets for reducing waste generation rates, recycling, and use of recycled content.

- **Perform environmental audits.** Currently most audits focus on potential Superfund cleanup liability or compliance with hazardous waste and employee health and safety regulations. For companies that primarily generate solid, non-hazardous waste, a study that matches waste generation and recycling rates to products or activities is likely to be more useful. Such an audit provides information for targeting waste reduction efforts.

- **Purchase more products with recycled content and, if applicable, recycled materials for manufacturing new products.** These efforts may necessitate new relationships with a diverse group of suppliers and thus alter inbound transportation practices.

- **Recycle or reuse a wide variety of materials, such as pallets, plastics, defective products, and process wastes from manufacturing and distribution centers.** Companies frequently must assume an active role in finding markets and arranging transportation for such materials.

- **Develop green products or services.** Companies begin to create, alter, or market products or services to respond to consumers' environmental attitudes. Efforts are typically focused on one or two items in a product line or a portfolio of services.

- **Assume responsibility for reusing and recycling products through industry coalitions and reverse distribution programs.** Through the American Plastics Council, for example, the plastics industry is funding the development of a recycling infrastructure by providing technical assistance to municipalities and by establishing independent plastics processing companies.

Organization

Proactive programs are typically launched with a commitment from the chief executive officer and other top management officials. One or two new managerial positions may be created to implement policy, identify new projects, and oversee internal recycling programs.

> ### *Environmental Management At Nike*
>
> *A five person Nike Environmental Action Team (NEAT) has full-time responsibility for waste reduction and compliance. NEAT emerged from monthly meetings of environmentally concerned employees who drafted Nike's environmental policy statement, promoted and received top management approval for a formal environmental department, and drafted the job descriptions. Their efforts are leveraged by 45 representatives worldwide. These volunteers coordinate the office paper and beverage container recycling program and funnel suggestions for improvements and special projects to the NEAT staff.*

Managers of new waste reduction programs have a variety of backgrounds. They may be selected from the area that is receiving the greatest public or government attention (e.g., packaging), has a strategic importance (e.g., merchandising), or is closest to the environmental issues (e.g., public affairs). Managerial slots may also be filled by an employee who has shown initiative in creating the program. In addition, the role of the waste reduction program in the firm's business strategy also influences the selection of managers and program organization. For example, at The Home Depot, where reuse and recycling complement and extend the firm's overall merchandising strategy, the manager of environmental affairs has a marketing background. Meanwhile, at The Coca-Cola Company, reuse and recycling programs are an off-shoot of the government affairs function and principally serve to lead and encourage local governments and vendors to take actions consistent with the company's existing product design and distribution system.

The emerging focus on new products and services in Phase 2 programs also extends responsibilities for waste reduction issues to new areas of the company. Interdepartmental committees may be formed to help gather data and establish priorities. In the companies studied in preparing this book, environmental affairs managers reported either formally or informally to such committees.

Resources

The resource commitments in Phase 2 remain modest. Companies frequently seek to leverage or avoid any major investments in new manufacturing equipment or distribution networks by joining industry coalitions and forming joint ventures with waste management companies. For example, The Home Depot formed a partnership with Mindis, a waste management firm, to create drop-off centers for construction and demolition debris. The Home Depot customers can bring this debris to drop-off centers located on The Home Depot grounds, which Mindis collects and recycles. In this way, The Home Depot was able to implement a recycling program with little investment.

Expanding a recycling program can involve some moderate expenditures for audits, equipment, and labor. Over the long term, labor costs for consolidating materials and operating balers are likely to be the most significant. Recycled product purchases, with the exception of office paper, may actually save money.

Reuse and Recycling

Most recycled materials, other than some plastics, are less expensive to purchase than virgin raw material, but require more processing to achieve comparable performance. Green product development costs are similar to any new product development costs, but may require extra research, especially for political sensitivities.

3.4 Phase 3: Value-Seeking Approach

In a 1990 speech to financial analysts, Procter & Gamble's Chairman and Chief Executive Officer, Edwin Artzt, identified environmental management as P&G's "greatest global challenge."

"Aggressive environmental management is essential if P&G is to continue to maintain the leadership position that the company has enjoyed in its product categories. We must anticipate and address environmental issues from the moment we conceive a product, all the way through product development, testing, manufacture, marketing, and sales, right up to the final moment when a satisfied customer disposes of an empty container."

This statement reveals that P&G's top officials are committed to making environmental concerns an issue throughout every aspect of the company and its products. Phase 3 programs require top management support and commitment and a thorough review of a company's environmental outlook.

Value-seeking programs assume that significant competitive advantage can be gained by developing a unique set of capabilities in environmental management. Phase 3 programs:

Program Goals

- **Integrate environmental activities into a business strategy that differentiates the company from competitors and creates new profit centers.** For example, each of DuPont's 35 strategic business units systematically analyzes its customers' operations to identify opportunities for DuPont to reclaim its products after use or to market new polymer products that use recycled materials.

- **Operate the company with the least possible environmental impact in accordance with sustainable development principles.** For example, Aveda Corporation, a hair care products and cosmetics manufacturer, has set a goal of managing operations to have a positive or equal impact on the earth. As one step toward that goal, the company plants an equivalent number of trees to replace the paper it uses each year.

Typical Activities

Phase 3 programs are marked by their breadth and their commitment to performance evaluation. Environmental impacts are measured, not assumed. Progress toward goals is tracked. Employees have direct incentives to ensure that policies are implemented. Typical Phase 3 activities include the following:

- **Use environmental life-cycle analysis to evaluate products and packaging.** Life-cycle studies compare emissions and resource consumption at all phases of a product's life from manufacture through disposal. They can provide a more complete picture of a product's environmental impacts than studies based on single attributes, such as recyclability.

- **Design products for disassembly and recycling or reuse.** To facilitate separating product components for recycling, IBM has reduced the number of polymers in its personal computer from 10 to one and U.S. auto manufacturers have set a goal of using only four or five different plastic polymers in future car designs.

- **Create competitive advantages through reverse distribution programs.** Through the use of third-party capital assets, strategic corporate investments in selected segments of the reverse supply chain, and in-sourcing, Xerox, DuPont, and other leading firms have been able to create significant competitive advantages with their reverse distribution programs. (The Xerox program is described in Chapter 6. DuPont's program is profiled in Chapter 8.)

- **Maximize the impact of waste reduction achievements by asking suppliers to commit to waste reduction goals.** Computer 2000, the third-largest distributor of computer hardware and software in the world, recently announced that it will sign contracts only with new vendors that offer "recyclable and environmentally friendly products."[5]

***Using Life-Cycle Analysis to Evaluate Recycling
and Reuse Initiatives[6]***

The logistics profession was a leader in developing life-cycle costing, a valuable technique for evaluating reuse and recycling programs. In 1965, the Logistics Management Institute prepared the path-breaking report entitled "Life Cycle Costing in Equipment Purchase" for the Assistant Secretary of Defense for Installations and Logistics. This report led to defense procurement improvements by recognizing the importance of considering costs over the lifetime of defense equipment and systems.

Life-cycle costing is useful for analyzing the value of reuse and recycling programs because it captures the multi-stage nature of these programs. "Life-cycle cost analysis requires thinking through and identifying all the cost-bearing activities associated with the item or system throughout its lifetime, from acquisition through disposal." For example, an analysis of the value of reusable containers as opposed to single use containers would include:

- The difference in purchase prices;
- The avoided purchase of single use containers;
- The difference in transportation costs;
- Any difference in materials handling costs;
- The avoided disposal costs;
- Any difference in recycling revenues; and
- The additional costs for repairing reusable containers.

Container quality and consumer reactions would also be important considerations.

Life-cycle analysis also estimates the environmental, as well as financial, costs and benefits of waste reduction programs. This application is less well established due to the wide range of potential environmental impacts, the lack of data on these impacts, and the difficulty of comparing different environmental impacts (e.g., water use, energy use, and carbon dioxide emissions). For single use versus reusable containers, a complete environmental life-cycle analysis would include all emissions generated and resources consumed during the

> **Using Life-Cycle Analysis to Evaluate Recycling
> and Reuse Initiatives (continued)**
>
> *production and transport of the major raw materials used to make the
> containers and the manufacture, distribution, use, reuse, recycling, and
> disposal of the containers. The analysis would ideally assess the
> relative environmental impacts of the emissions and resource
> consumption.*
>
> *While protocols for life-cycle assessments are still being developed
> by the U.S. Environmental Protection Agency and other parties, it is
> important to note that the environmental benefits of recycling and reuse
> projects will eventually be subject to scrutiny. A reverse distribution
> and remanufacturing program that results in greater energy use and
> related emissions than a forward distribution system could make a firm
> vulnerable to the public ire and regulation that it was trying to avoid by
> initiating the program.*

- **Develop internal incentives and enforcement mechanisms.** Companies directly encourage employees to be more environmentally conscious. Browning-Ferris, a major international waste services company, ties the bonuses of district landfill managers to their scores on a 100-point scale of environmental, health, and safety goals. Managers that do not pass do not receive a bonus, regardless of how much money they make for the company.[7]

- **Critically review and reassess all existing processes, products, and services.** Identify opportunities for greater materials and toxicity reduction, reuse, and/or recycling. Environmental costs can be incorporated into accounting systems to charge departments for waste produced internally and

wastes produced by a company's products. Monitor
new environmental developments and change goals
and systems as necessary.

Few companies have implemented all of these activities, although
firms such as DuPont, Xerox, Procter & Gamble, and Aveda are
on their way.

Organization

At companies with Phase 3 programs, responsibility for waste
reduction is spread widely throughout the organization. The
chief executive officer or other top corporate officer establishes a
high level of environmental commitment. Interdepartmental
teams help set policies and identify opportunities for
improvement. Waste reduction managers coordinate and help
implement policies throughout the firm. New divisions may be
established to create reverse distribution programs or manage
company-wide recycling efforts. Moreover, each department is
expected and encouraged to contribute new ideas and initiatives
to help the company meet its environmental goals. In these
ways, a firm may be able to develop new procedures and
products that will lead to higher profits.

Resources

The total costs of Phase 3 waste reduction activities are
difficult to calculate because they are integral to the company's
operations and cut across department lines. Generally, firms
with Phase 3 programs limit their capital exposure by relying on
the assets of third parties, particularly when they are initially
testing new markets. They out-source activities where they lack

any strategic advantages and use in-house resources to take advantage of proprietary competencies.

In some instances large investments have been beneficial for leading companies. Procter & Gamble, for example, has committed $20 million to promote solid waste composting programs. The money is used to sponsor several composting trade associations, technical assistance for municipalities, and demonstration projects. P&G's high level of visibility and active participation in solid waste issues have been helpful to the company. By participating in CONEG's packaging initiatives (see section 2.4), for example, P&G's corporate policy concerning the maximum acceptable concentration of certain metals in packaging has been reflected in model legislation.

3.5 Implications for Logistics Personnel

Logistics personnel have been only minimally involved in reuse and recycling programs despite strong conceptual arguments for their involvement in designing and implementing such programs. The review of reuse and recycling program development suggests, however, that as these programs mature, the initiatives that affect logistics personnel or demand their expertise will multiply. The relatively fluid nature of the organizational structure surrounding waste reduction programs also indicates that logisticians could enter these new functions relatively easily.

Of the 17 companies interviewed, those that had the greatest level of logistics involvement in reuse and recycling programs, DuPont, North American Van Lines, and Xerox, had each made significant commitments to Phase 2 and Phase 3 activities.

These companies either initiated reverse distribution systems for their products (DuPont and Xerox) or supplied reverse distribution services to others (North American Van Lines). Logistics personnel, with their knowledge of distribution systems and their ability to balance the needs of several departments to derive a best solution, were tapped to establish or manage these reverse distribution channels.

By definition, Phase 2 and Phase 3 programs extend responsibility for achieving waste reduction goals to employees throughout the company. Thus, even if a firm does not start a dramatic new product take-back program, managers in all divisions will be expected to help the firm meet recycling goals and identify opportunities for improvement. Logistics personnel have the opportunity to differentiate themselves from other operations managers by advocating environmental initiatives and finding ways to implement them to reduce costs and increase revenues. (Chief executive officers committed to waste reduction programs often cite the attitudes of middle managers within their firms as one of the biggest obstacles to program implementation.[8])

Conversely, logistics managers who do not actively participate in developing environmental programs may find themselves responsible for addressing difficulties created by poor planning decisions, such as disputing liability for damaged products with carriers due to inappropriately reduced packaging or processing recyclables at warehouses that were not designed to handle them.

As noted in Section 3.2, individuals with full-time responsibility for reuse and recycling programs come from a variety of backgrounds. In this respect, reuse and recycling program management is much more open to logistics personnel than environmental compliance programs that tend to rely on the expertise of scientists, engineers, and lawyers. Reuse and recycling are also transportation intensive operations, which could give logisticians an advantage over other professionals.

Opportunities to tackle reuse and recycling full-time, however, are extremely limited at most companies. Many companies interviewed for this study seemed to derive the energy for their reuse and recycling programs from a single manager, who borrowed resources from other corporate activity centers to launch projects. While such a manager may eventually gain a larger staff, many companies contract with third-party service providers and work through trade associations, rather than build large in-house departments. The adage that "whenever a company produces something internally that others can buy or produce more efficiently, it sacrifices competitive advantage" appears to apply extensively in reuse and recycling program design.

3.6 Case Study: Implementing Waste Reduction at McDonald's[9]

The evolution of waste reduction programs at McDonald's Corporation illustrates how a company progresses from reacting to environmental issues to developing a proactive and value seeking program. McDonald's approach to waste reduction is consistent with the company's policy of systematically identifying, testing, and evaluating all innovations to ensure their compatibility with the company's carefully choreographed system for operating quick service restaurants.

McDonald's visibility as the nation's leading fast food firm has placed it in the center of several environmental controversies. In the 1970s, the company was engaged in debates about roadside litter -- the company has always emphasized litter prevention in its operating instructions for franchises. More recently, McDonald's has developed policies to respond to public concerns about depletion of the ozone layer and the destruction of tropical rain forests. Waste reduction, however, has become the company's top environmental issue.

McDonald's is continually seeking ways to improve the quality, efficiency, and profitability of its restaurants. This philosophy is especially apparent in the company's approach to packaging procurement. Over the last two decades the company has adopted a number of new packages based on their ability to reduce materials usage and to preserve the quality of the prepared foods. For example, a typical restaurant meal of a Big Mac, fries, and a shake uses 46 percent less packaging today than it did in the 1970s.

The company originally switched from a paper wrap to polystyrene in the 1970s because the polystyrene offered better insulation for the sandwiches. Negative public opinion about polystyrene packaging in the 1980s served as a catalyst to raise the importance of waste reduction issues at McDonald's. As a major user of polystyrene packaging, McDonald's Corporation was the target of grassroots groups that wanted to ban the material for its perceived negative environmental impact. Several communities had already enacted bans on polystyrene packaging.

In the late 1980s, McDonald's headquarters assigned 10 people to a corporate environmental affairs department to design and implement a polystyrene recycling program at its restaurants. This staff was supplemented by full-time regional coordinators. At that time, post-consumer polystyrene recycling was just beginning; the first polystyrene processing center had just been opened by a consortium of plastics industry firms in Massachusetts.

In October 1989, shortly after the pilot tests for polystyrene recycling had begun, McDonald's accepted an offer from the Environmental Defense Fund (EDF) to participate in a dialogue about its materials use and recycling policies. After a series of meetings between the CEO of McDonald's and the Executive Director of EDF, the two organizations agreed to form a joint waste reduction task force to explore waste reduction options for McDonald's restaurants.

In November 1991, before the EDF plan was released, McDonald's announced a phase out of polystyrene by replacing its hamburger clamshell with a paper-based wrapping with a polyethylene liner and withdrawing from the polystyrene recycling program. The decision created considerable controversy, because McDonald's was replacing a recyclable material with a source-reduced but non-recyclable wrapper.

The decision was partly based on problems with the polystyrene recycling program and the environmental attributes of the new wrapper. The polystyrene recycling program had not been running smoothly for a number of reasons, including:

◆ Contamination of materials;

◆ Low volumes, since most customers use McDonald's take-out service and therefore do not leave waste in the restaurant;

◆ High costs of transportation and processing; and

◆ Permitting problems for the processing facility.

The new paper-based wrapper performed comparably to the clamshell. Although it could not be recycled, it used 70 to 90 percent less material for primary packaging and close to 90 percent less material for shipping packaging. EDF evaluated the two packaging options, using data from a life-cycle analysis of the two materials, and concluded that the paper wrapper was the best packaging from an environmental perspective.

The McDonald's-EDF partnership concluded in April 1991 with the release of a 42 item waste reduction action plan. As of April 30, 1992, McDonald's had completed 19 of the 42 initiatives, 12 initiatives were in progress, and the remaining items were of an ongoing nature. In addition, McDonald's added 20 new initiatives to the list in 1992. The majority of items in the plan involved redesigning packaging and food service items to reduce the amount of materials used. The recycling and composting and reuse initiatives are summarized in the box below. Items that affect restaurant operations are adopted nationwide only if they survive McDonald's rigorous system of lab tests, small in-store tests, and regional multi-store tests.

McDonald's Waste Reduction Action Items

Recycling and Composting

- Implementing corrugated recycling at all restaurants (goal)
- Testing the feasibility of composting organic waste from restaurants
- Testing a co-mingled waste recycling program in Southern California
- Establishing a pilot program for LDPE plastic recycling
- Establishing a program to spend at least $100 million worth of recycled products annually
- Establishing TRIACE, an independent company to centralize the purchase of waste collection and recycling services at restaurants
- Continuing to research new packaging designs that enhance the package's recyclability or compostability

Reuse

- Evaluating the use of reusable coffee filters
- Evaluating a reusable lid for salads and breakfast entrees
- Testing replacement of corrugated containers with reusable plastic containers for meat and poultry deliveries
- Testing reusable shipping containers for ketchup packets
- Developing a more durable shipping pallet with Chep USA
- Testing a refillable coffee mug

Recycling at McDonald's is constrained by the contamination of many recyclables with food waste and the expense of collecting and finding markets for the low volumes of recyclables that restaurants generate. McDonald's hoped to overcome these problems and save on waste collection costs by centralizing its waste management system. (Traditionally, individual franchise operators procured their own waste management services.)

In the spring of 1990, McDonald's headquarters tapped a former distributor to form TRIACE, an independent company that would negotiate waste management and recycling services for

McDonald's restaurants. TRIACE worked to link contracts for waste collection to the less profitable recycling collection routes and negotiated with companies that could provide end markets for the recyclables recovered from McDonald's restaurants. The company's revenues were derived from service fees from restaurant operators and revenues from the sale of recyclable materials. TRIACE was not successful, however, in part due to the primacy of local relationships in waste management and the depressed market prices for recyclables in the early 1990s.

McDonald's corporate environmental group was downsized after the company withdrew from the polystyrene recycling program. With this change and as a result of the partnership with EDF, responsibility for implementing waste reduction is now spread widely throughout the company and even extends to McDonald's suppliers. Now two people handle Environmental Affairs at headquarters:

(1) The Department Director, who serves as an environmental ombudsman, makes decisions on restaurant waste reduction projects, and reports directly to the firm's Board of Directors; and

(2) A staff member, who responds to public requests for information and administers McDonald's recycled products procurement program.

Although the Environmental Affairs Department makes waste reduction policy decisions, four other departments are involved in testing and implementing waste reduction initiatives:

Reuse and Recycling

♦ The Product Development Department and the Operations Department set directions for improvements and changes in McDonald's menu and operations and test new packaging.

♦ The Quality Assurance Department sets and enforces purchasing specifications.

♦ The Purchasing Department works directly with suppliers and helps evaluate compliance.

Two cross-departmental teams have also been formed to identify waste reduction opportunities.

♦ The Optimum Packaging Team reviews opportunities to reduce and/or eliminate secondary and shipping packaging.

♦ The McRecycle Team identifies new applications for recycled content materials in every area of the company's business.

Restaurant operators can look to one of McDonald's 40 Regional Environmental Affairs Coordinators for assistance with waste reduction issues. These coordinators usually have distinguished themselves in other areas or have demonstrated a personal environmental commitment. They are asked to add environmental program tasks to their other duties, yet they do not receive an increase in salary for the added responsibilities. Their functions vary depending on the region of the country; areas with high waste disposal fees and most stringent recycling laws make the greatest demands on coordinators' time.

Participation in waste reduction programs has been included in performance reviews for outside contractors. All suppliers were asked to reduce their waste by 15 percent and to document the reductions in reports for McDonald's. Environmental goals have also been incorporated into audits of field distributors. McDonald's requires that its suppliers include 35 percent recycled material in corrugated shipping cartons. Packaging is now evaluated on waste reduction criteria, in addition to performance, cost, and availability.

Key Findings

✓ Corporate responses to pro-environmental attitudes and regulations can be viewed as progressing through three phases, from reactive to proactive to value-seeking.

✓ Each phase of the process is more comprehensive than the previous phase, reflecting both increasing corporate commitment to environmental goals and the realization that strategic benefits can be derived from environmental programs.

✓ Responsibility for managing the firm's program varies by program phase. Reactive programs may be managed by individuals who take initiative or by a government relations or environmental compliance team. Proactive programs may require the creation of one or two managerial positions. Value-seeking programs use managers for coordination, but integrate responsibility throughout the firm.

✓ The need for logistics personnel increases with the program's sophistication.

✓ Resource implications of environmental programs are difficult to estimate because mature programs cut across many sections of a firm.

Endnotes

1. Companies interviewed include Aveda, Bristol-Myers Squibb, Chep USA, DuPont, The Home Depot, McDonald's, Mindis Recycling, Nike, North American Van Lines, Owens Illinois, Procter & Gamble, RE-SOURCE AMERICA INC., Scientific

---

Certification Systems, Sears, Waste Management Inc., Xerox, and Zytec.

2. Karen Blumenfeld, Ralph Earle III, and Frank Annigbofer, "Environmental Performance and Business Strategy," *Prism*, Fourth Quarter, 1992, pages 65-81; Richard Monty, "Beyond Environmental Compliance: Business Strategies for Competitive Advantage," *Environmental Finance*, Spring 1991, page 4; Christopher Hart and Ellen Austen, "Proactive Environmental Management: Avoiding the Toxic Trap," *Sloan Management Review*, Winter 1990, page 9.

3. William Rathje and Cullen Murphy, *Rubbish! The Archaeology of Garbage, What Our Garbage Tells Us About Ourselves*, Harper Collins Publishers, Inc., New York, NY, 1992, pages 113-114.

4. Ann B. Graham et al., *Managing the Global Environmental Challenge*, prepared and published by Business International and Arthur D. Little, New York, NY, 1992, page 228.

5. "German Computer Distributor Wants to Work with 'Green' Vendors," *Business and the Environment*, September 1992, page 9.

6. Paul E. Bailey, "Life-Cycle Costing and Pollution Prevention," *Pollution Prevention Review*, Winter 1990-91, page 27.

7. Ann B. Graham et al., *Managing the Global Environmental Challenge*, page 214.

8. Managers may oppose these programs because they often believe that the costs of environmental programs will not be able

to be passed on to consumers. See Pieter Winsemius and Ulrich Guntram, "Responding to the Environmental Challenge," *Business Horizons*, March/April 1992, page 19.

9. The primary sources for this article were *Final Report, McDonald's Corporation and Environmental Defense Fund Waste Reduction Task Force*, April 1991; George C. Lodge and Jeffrey Rayport, "Knee-deep and Rising: America's Recycling Crisis," *Harvard Business Review*, September/October 1991; and *McDonald's Waste Reduction Action Plan, Status Report*, April 1, 1992.

INBOUND LOGISTICS: RECYCLING SUPPLY CHAINS

4

4.1 Introduction

Procuring recycled materials or products with recycled content can pose unique control and management challenges for manufacturers. The difficulties are likely to be most acute for industries and firms that are using recycled materials collected in new municipal recycling programs. Segments of the glass, paper, and metals industries, however, have a long history of using recycled materials and are supplied by a well established network of scrap dealers and secondary materials processors. For companies in these industry segments, the critical issues are not how to set up a supply chain for recycled materials, but how to adapt to the new market conditions created by the influx of recyclables from municipal solid waste (MSW) collection programs. The logistics associated with procuring and using recycled materials are more significant when the materials are direct inputs into the manufacturing process, as opposed to products used to support general business functions (e.g., recycled content office paper).

Supply chains differ for reused products and recycling. Most reused products are exchanged among end-users and, if necessary, are refurbished at the retail level. Thus, they rarely travel through reverse distribution channels to manufacturers. In contrast, recycled products become raw materials for manufacturing. In addition, there are few public collection systems for reuse, whereas state and local governments commonly operate or sponsor recycling programs.

Product reuse typically consists of exchanges between users, such as handing down old clothing and furniture within a family or exchanging office equipment, furnishings, and used computer equipment through third parties. The Salvation Army, Goodwill stores, and Junior League shops have long facilitated product reuse between less closely connected parties. Antique dealers and some appliance retailers purchase used products, perform any needed repairs, and then resell them. Product parts may also be reused. Automobile junkyards, for example, have long been a source for car parts.

Product and packaging reuse affect inbound supply chains for manufacturers in two situations:

(1) When manufacturers retrieve their products or component parts from customers, remanufacture the products or components, and then market them. These reverse distribution systems are discussed in Chapter 6.

(2) When shipping packaging is recirculated among manufacturers, distributors, and retailers. The reuse of shipping packaging is closely related to efforts to reduce and recycle wastes from the distribution process. The next chapter on forward distribution discusses the design of reusable containers. Chapter 6 describes how reusable packaging systems work.

Because the issues of product reuse are best addressed in later chapters, this chapter focuses on the recycling aspects of inbound supply chains.

This chapter is organized as follows:

♦ Section 4.2 provides an overview of the traditional recycling industry.

♦ Section 4.3 discusses the new supply chains that recover recyclables from the municipal solid waste stream and how they affect traditional recyclers.

♦ Section 4.4 identifies the potential value of buying recycled materials.

♦ Section 4.5 portrays key logistics issues associated with the purchase of recycled material from municipal recycling programs.

♦ Section 4.6 briefly reviews the procurement process for finished goods with recycled content.

♦ Section 4.7 discusses the importance of closer relations among participants in the secondary materials supply chain.

♦ Finally, section 4.8 describes two case studies of manufacturers: one firm purchases recycled materials to make packaging; the other buys recycled content packaging.

4.2 The Scrap Recycling Infrastructure

The flurry of enthusiasm over municipal recycling programs has tended to overshadow the extensive network of scrap dealers already operating in the United States. In fact, all industrial scrap recyclers processed over 98 million tons of material in 1990.[1]

In contrast, the U.S. Environmental Protection Agency (EPA) reported that 33.4 million tons of municipal waste were recycled and composted in 1990.[2] The difference between the two figures is primarily due to EPA's exclusion of metal fabricating scrap, automobiles, and paper cuttings, which EPA does not regard as municipal waste.

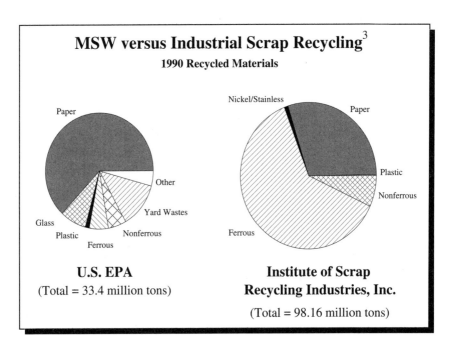

MSW versus Industrial Scrap Recycling[3]

1990 Recycled Materials

U.S. EPA
(Total = 33.4 million tons)

Institute of Scrap Recycling Industries, Inc.
(Total = 98.16 million tons)

The scrap industry tends to be organized by material type. Most processors handle a particular type of material, such as ferrous metal or paper, but depending on local conditions, a scrap dealer might occasionally take other materials as well. Scrap dealers negotiate for materials with local businesses and waste haulers. The dealers may pick-up large quantities of material from a single location, but usually the recyclables must be brought to them. They typically sort and process (e.g., bale) the recyclables before selling them to other processors or manufacturers. Most firms in the scrap industry are independent businesses, rather than affiliates of manufacturers or large waste management firms. Three examples of these supply chains are provided below.

(1) A network of ferrous metal processors and shredders process and manufacture scrap into prepared grades for melting at a steel smelter or other melting facility.

(2) Paper brokers handle corrugated cardboard and office paper from large commercial sources, sort them by grade, and sell them to deinking plants or mills that manufacture paperboard, tissue, wallboard, and newsprint. (Newspaper and tissue mills need deinked material; paperboard and wallboard manufacturers do not.) While deinking plants are often owned by virgin mills, some companies are building independent facilities to serve manufacturers in a particular region. Some of the major paper manufacturers, such as Weyerhauser and Stone Container, have their own collection and brokerage divisions.

(3) About 200 small grease recycling companies collect 1.2 million tons of congealed grease from restaurants each year, process it to remove food scraps, and sell most of it to the rendering industry for making animal feed and small amounts to steel companies for lubricating sheet steel. The grease recycling industry has roots going back to the 1950s, when fried food first became popular on restaurant menus.[4]

These recycling markets have developed because collecting and processing metal, paper, and grease to make new products provide a clear economic benefit to the companies involved. Environmental concerns and recycling legislation generally have not been motivating factors. Because the materials that have been recovered through these traditional recycling supply chains tend to be homogenous, they do not require intensive and costly processing to remove contaminants.

4.3 Growth of Municipal Recycling Programs

State recycling laws enacted over the last five years have spurred the development of numerous municipal recycling programs. Since local governments have historically had more control over residential as opposed to commercial waste collection, local recycling programs have typically consisted of curbside collection of bottles, cans and newsprint from single family homes. Between 1988 and 1992, the number of curbside recycling programs grew by more than 500 percent. They now number more than 5400.[5] In the few states with mandatory recycling for businesses, companies are commonly required to contract directly with private companies for recycling, as they do for waste collection. Local governments, however, may attempt to exert more control over commercial recycling once their residential programs are established, particularly where commercial wastes are disposed of in municipal landfills.

Prior to the onslaught of state recycling legislation in the past few years, municipal solid waste (MSW) recycling consisted of independently coordinated, low technology endeavors. Consumers brought beverage containers to industry sponsored buy-back centers or retail stores as required by bottle bills. Volunteer groups often collected newspaper for fundraising efforts. Some large companies had office paper recycling programs and the grocery industry recycled large amounts of corrugated cardboard.

MSW Recycling Supply Chain Structure

The new municipal recycling programs have spawned a supply chain with four links: collectors, sorters, processors, and manufacturers. Local governments and private companies may fulfill more than one role in the supply chain. Municipalities often collect recyclables and build sorting facilities. The four largest domestic waste management companies, Waste Management Inc., Browning Ferris Industries, Laidlaw Inc., and Attwoods, PLC, all have collection and sorting operations and are adding links to processors and remanufacturers. Some paper manufacturers own companies that collect and sort high grade office paper.

Collectors. Recycling collection systems differ for private homes and businesses. Residential recyclables are collected by local governments or private waste services companies that have contracts with cities to serve a certain number of homes.

Commercial recyclables are almost always collected by the private sector, with collectors and generators signing individual contracts. Within the waste industry, the larger waste management companies have been more likely than smaller firms to provide recycling services. For example, the seven largest publicly held companies (Attwoods, Browning Ferris, Chambers Development Co., Inc., Laidlaw, Mid-American Waste Systems, Waste Management, and Western Waste Industries) collect the majority of the residential recyclables handled by the private sector even though they only control 30 percent of the total waste services market.[6]

Sorters. Sorters receive recyclables from collectors or waste generators. Depending on the type of material and market conditions, they may pay for the recyclables or charge a sorting fee. MSW recycling has spawned a new type of sorting facility, known as a materials recovery facility or MRF. More than 190 MRFs are now operating in the country. Most MRFs were built primarily to separate beverage containers, bale newsprint, and otherwise handle mixed waste from residential collection programs. A few facilities are now moving to handle commercial wastes (primarily paper) as well. These plants can range from extremely low-tech operations where recyclables are dumped on a warehouse floor and sorted by hand to totally mechanized plants that sort recyclables via magnets, blowers, screens, and other devices. Most MRFs use a combination of manual and mechanical sorting. They usually charge a tipping fee or operate under a municipal service contract.

Processors. Most processors are dedicated to a particular materials type, although some processing functions are performed at MRFs. Processors buy sorted recyclables and transform them into raw materials, which they sell to manufacturers. Examples include paper deinking facilities, glass beneficiation plants, and plastic washing, flaking, extruding, and pelletizing facilities. At this stage, the recyclables are often called secondary materials to distinguish them from virgin raw materials.

Recyclable materials may be sent to a series of processors, with each one adding additional refinements. Processing facilities are sometimes owned by virgin materials manufacturers. The degree of this vertical integration varies by industry. For example, the paper industry is more integrated than the plastics industry.

Remanufacturers. Remanufacturers combine secondary material with virgin materials to make products with recycled content. The steel and paper industries are the largest consumers of recycled material. In 1992, the steel industry consumed 45,930,000 tons of recycled scrap; the paper industry consumed 27,299,000 tons of domestic scrap.[7] Examples of products with recycled content include automobiles, newspapers, tissue paper, boxboard, glass bottles, wallboard, carpets, and lubricating oil.

The current logistical issues associated with recycling relate primarily to inefficiencies in collecting, sorting, processing, and remanufacturing the materials recovered from curbside collection programs, and to a lesser extent, the recyclables recovered from businesses.

Relationship Between MSW Recyclers and Scrap Dealers

The new municipal recycling programs threaten to disrupt traditional recycling supply chains that depend on scrap dealers. Since municipalities are recycling primarily to comply with regulatory mandates and to divert materials from landfills, they have been relatively insensitive to price signals. Thus local governments have continued to send recyclables to market even when prices for them are negative, which drives prices even lower. Scrap dealers, who are in business to make a profit, are affected by the influx of materials from municipal programs. They sell to the same processors and end users as MSW recyclers, but traditionally handle higher grades of material.

The price pressures on scrap dealers combined with the need to improve the economies of scale at MRFs may be bringing the scrap dealers and the municipal waste recyclers closer together. For example, the fourth largest waste collection company in the world, Attwoods, which operates municipal recycling programs, recently purchased Mindis, a major scrap dealer with a hub and spoke network of drop-off centers and processing facilities in the southeastern United States. Partnerships with scrap dealers are attractive to municipal waste recyclers because the material that dealers handle, such as metal scrap, can "subsidize" the sorting of less valuable household recyclables.

In other cases, local government attempts to increase the efficiency of MSW recycling by controlling the flow of recyclable materials have the potential to supplant scrap dealers entirely.

♦ In California, some local governments have begun to grant exclusive franchises to waste services firms for collecting commercial recyclables similar to franchises granted for residential recyclables. Franchises offer the benefits of centralization, which can be significant from a routing and recordkeeping standpoint. The drawback of franchise agreements is that they essentially create monopolies.[8]

♦ Local governments frequently enact flow control laws that require all non-segregated recyclables to be taken to the new county-owned processing facility, presumably to help secure financing for the facility.

Both of these types of flow control laws are being challenged in court.

The pressure on dealers has several ramifications for manufacturers that buy recycled materials. For manufacturers that purchase only recycled materials, the competition has created a temporary bonanza of bargains in secondary materials markets. Vertically integrated manufacturers that own scrap dealers and processors, however, may be negatively affected.

Market pressures may continue to favor the mergers of scrap dealers with large waste services companies. Companies now supplied by the small independent brokers may later be served by national, vertically integrated companies.

4.4 The Value of Buying Recycled

Buying recyclable materials and finished products with recycled content can have both financial and environmental benefits. Much of the financial savings are indirect, and relate to complying with existing minimum content laws (e.g., avoiding fines) and preempting the cost of complying with new mandatory minimum content laws through voluntary efforts to buy recycled products. In some cases, however, using recycled feedstock leads to lower capital and operating costs for manufacturing facilities. The environmental benefits from "buying recycled" can include resource conservation and reductions in energy consumption and pollutants produced during manufacturing.

The push to buy recycled products is largely a reaction to the minimum content laws already enacted for newspapers, telephone books, and packaging material and the threat of additional state and federal laws. Thus, a primary source of value from buying recycled is compliance with existing laws.

Minimum content legislation that mandates recycled content levels for specific products can be extremely inefficient from a manufacturing perspective. For example, in 1991 and 1992 the California Legislature considered a minimum content requirement for steel cans (Assembly Bill 1423). More steel is recycled than any other material, but most of it goes into manufacturing automobiles, appliances, and steel beams for construction. The production of sheet metal for cans uses a different manufacturing process, which can use only limited amounts of post-consumer scrap. Thus, the proposed legislation could have caused severe dislocations in the steel industry without increasing overall steel recycling rates.

Recycled material is usually less expensive to purchase than comparable virgin inputs, although the need to remove contaminants adds costs to using recycled materials. For products that are relatively impervious to contaminants, such as paperboard, which can be made from multiple grades of non-deinked paper, the use of secondary materials lowers processing costs and saves energy. A recent EPA report estimates that "there are a number of instances in which the cost of producing deinked pulp would be lower than the cost to produce virgin pulp," primarily due to a more than 10-fold savings in energy costs from the deinking process.[10]

Lower Environmental Impacts for Secondary Materials[9]	
Material	*Estimated $/Ton Impact*
Boxboard	
– virgin	382
– recycled	247
Aluminum	
– virgin	1,963
– recycled	342
Glass	
– virgin	157
– recycled	127

Depending on the manufacturing process, the use of recycled material can also reduce air and water emissions. A recent study by the Tellus Institute, a Boston-based non-profit environmental research group, assigned a per ton cost to the environmental impact of various packaging materials based on the costs to control pollutants generated during the product's lifecycle. Where enough data were available to compare packages made from 100 percent virgin material versus recycled material, the costs were generally lower for the recycled products.[11] The study also found that the lightest weight packaging products, such as polyethylene terephalate (PET) soda bottles and aseptic juice boxes, usually have the fewest environmental impacts of any packaging type.

4.5 Buying Recycled Material from MSW Collection Programs

Manufacturers procuring recycled materials for the first time or dramatically increasing their purchases often must alter transportation networks and materials handling procedures. Companies may also restructure their supply chains to address regulatory pressures or capture financial benefits. For the plastics industry, buying recycled material has also involved working with local governments to develop a collection and processing infrastructure. Since pressure to use recycled materials is likely to continue, companies that adjust their supply chains to efficiently obtain recycled materials will have an edge over their competitors.

The following issues are critical to developing inbound supply chains for recyclable materials.

Numerous Suppliers

The recycling supply chain starts with many generators and collectors of recyclable materials and narrows considerably as recyclables are processed and remanufactured or exported. The disparity between the large number of suppliers of recycled materials and the small number of purchasers within local markets, which are constrained by transportation costs, creates a demand driven market. When suppliers are motivated by regulatory as opposed to economic incentives, the secondary materials market can quickly become glutted with recyclables as new laws are enacted. This supply structure also limits the ease of vertical integration in the recycling industry as compared to industries that produce virgin raw materials.

Limited Capacity of Individual Suppliers

Secondary materials processors often have limited supply capacity relative to suppliers of virgin materials. Thus, in developing secondary materials supply chains, purchasers often must rely on several sources. For example, when Owens Brockway started purchasing recycled plastic resin for manufacturing containers, the company had to purchase material from multiple processors to obtain needed quantities. (See section 4.8.) Bulk shipments may not be available, at least until the recycling infrastructure is more mature.

Transportation and Handling Costs

Transportation costs and handling costs can quickly exceed the value of recycled materials; thus, reducing these costs is vital to profitable recycling. Transport costs are affected by the distance between sources of recyclables and manufacturers, as described in the next paragraph, and the fact that recyclables often remain commingled with non-recyclables as they travel through several links in the supply chain. Some manufacturers, for example, require recyclables to be delivered intact, so that they can more easily screen out contaminants. In other cases, recyclables are not densified because the volumes of materials handled by MRFs or commercial generators do not justify the costs of purchasing and operating the balers, granulators, and other equipment.

Location of Supplies in Urban Areas

The purchase of recycled material may change inbound transportation patterns. Virgin materials extraction and processing industries are often located in remote areas where large forests and productive mines remain. The petrochemical industry is concentrated along the Gulf of Mexico. In contrast, recyclables, which are sometimes called "urban ore," are most plentiful in metropolitan areas.

To reduce transport distances, manufacturing facilities that use significant quantities of recycled materials may move closer to recycled material supplies. While processors have quickly sprung up near cities, relocating capital intensive manufacturing capacity is considerably more difficult. Relocation is especially problematic in industries without rapid growth, because building new plants requires closing other plants dedicated to virgin capacity. Siting new manufacturing facilities is further complicated by public opposition; public support for recycling does not always translate into support for living next to manufacturing facilities that use secondary materials.

Uncertain Supplies

Using secondary materials in manufacturing may require lengthening delivery lead times to compensate for uncertain supplies, with the result that inventories increase. Since many municipal collection programs are highly subsidized by state funds, these programs might be cut back or discontinued during state budget crises. So far, however, these programs have resulted in excess supplies, not shortages of recyclables. Supplies are probably the least stable for materials that are just being added to collection programs, such as plastics and mixed paper.

Quality Concerns

Much of the current publicity about recycled products stresses that they are of equal quality to virgin products. These claims can be made because processors implement extensive quality control procedures to screen out contaminants from recyclables. The potential for damage from contaminants, however, can remain high. For example, resin from just one PVC bottle can change the melting point of an entire batch of PET resin. Thus, more extensive quality control systems and new materials specifications for recyclable materials may be needed. As noted above, some manufacturers specify that deliveries of recyclables should be intact so they can more easily identify contaminants.

> ### *Restructured Newsprint Supply Chain*
>
> *In industries where recycled material is beginning to comprise a significant percentage of inputs, the supply chain may be largely restructured. For example, minimum content laws for newsprint have tipped the balance of newsprint production from Canadian mills located in remote areas next to large forests to U.S. mills operating near large cities. When states began enacting recycled content mandates for newspapers in the late 1980s, Canadian mills had just one deinking plant, while U.S. mills had eight such plants. Newspaper publishers switched to the U.S. suppliers, who also began siting additional facilities near urban areas.*
>
> *To prevent massive erosion of their customer base, the Canadian producers have been slowing or eliminating production at virgin mills and building deinking capacity. For raw materials, the Canadian mills are importing old newsprint by rail from the Midwest and Northeast United States.*

4.6 Buying Finished Products with Recycled Content

The primary barriers to increased procurement of recycled products are questions about availability, performance, and cost. While these factors are all influenced by the logistics of recovering recyclable material, procurement of finished goods with recycled content, either for general business use or as an input to manufacturing, generally involves few changes in inbound transportation or materials handling procedures. The inbound supply chain disruptions are almost entirely borne by processors and primary manufacturers because these companies deal directly with scrap generators, collectors, and sorters -- the new links in the supply chain.

Availability

Reacting to the threat of additional minimum content legislation and increased corporate environmental awareness, many large companies are requesting their suppliers to incorporate recycled content into their products. Only limited quantities of these new products are available initially. The supply, however, gradually increases with continued demand by large corporations and then by smaller companies that lack the purchasing clout to force changes on their own. The demand for products with recycled content increases the demand for secondary materials, which helps develop the recycling infrastructure.

The availability of products with recycled content has increased dramatically over the last few years. More recycled products are now being sold through traditional office supply catalogues and paper companies. An emerging variety of

---

specialty retailers and mail order companies focus on environmentally friendly products. Businesses are also sharing information on recycled products and sources via computer data bases and industry associations. Many firms, however, are not aware of the variety of available recycled products or where they can be ordered.

Corporate procurement programs typically obtain recycled content copy and printing paper. Other products with recycled content include coated paper, pencils, desk supplies, lubricant oil, organic mulch, and many construction materials. In addition, aluminum cans, cereal boxes, glass bottles, and automobiles all contain significant quantities of recycled material, although few people think of these products as "recycled."

The consistency of the supply of products with recycled content is also a concern, particularly to firms that purchase products made from secondary materials that are just now being added to many collection programs (e.g., plastics, juice boxes,

---

McDonald's Recycled Product Procurement

McDonald's established the McRecycle USA program in 1990 to promote the purchase of recycled content products. McDonald's set a goal of spending at least $100 million annually on recycled products for its restaurants, which is about 25 percent of expenditures on building and remodeling restaurants. In the first two years, McDonald's purchased more than $400 million of recycled paper products and other recycled products used in building, remodeling, and operating its restaurants. Vendors can call 1-800-220-3809 on Monday through Friday from 9:00 to 5:00 EST to register their products for McDonald's certification. McDonald's environmental affairs department also makes this list of vendors available to other interested parties.

and mixed paper). The ability of collection programs to efficiently and profitably recover and process these items remains clouded.

The Buy Recycled Business Alliance

In September 1992, 25 major U.S. companies joined The Buy Recycled Business Alliance to stimulate increased purchases of recycled products by the business community. The Alliance hopes to recruit another 5,000 members by the end of 1994. The Alliance has three main goals:

(1) Requiring suppliers to make products with higher recycled content levels;

(2) Helping businesses identify available recycled products; and

(3) Exchanging information about recycled product prices and performance.

Each Alliance member has agreed to conduct a benchmark survey of its procurement practices and contribute to an annual report of the group's collective progress in buying recycled.

The Alliance is administered by the National Recycling Coalition, a non-profit recycling advocacy group with a diverse membership of industry professionals and environmentalists. Initial funding was provided through grants from the U.S. EPA, Waste Management Incorporated, and others. The 1993 budget of $325,000 for staff expenses, 20 workshops, and publications, will be provided entirely by member companies.

Performance

Questions about the performance or quality of recycled products has long been cited as an impediment to the demand

---

for these products. While virgin and secondary materials often have clear quality differences, the differences in products using these inputs are likely to be negligible. The best way to resolve questions about quality, as with any product, is to test its performance before purchasing large quantities.

Cost

Recycled products can be more expensive than products made entirely from virgin materials, depending in part on the maturity of the material recovery channel. In industries that have developed economies of scale in recycling, recycled products can be less expensive than virgin products. In contrast, recycled copy paper and coated free sheet paper can be significantly more expensive than their virgin fiber counterparts because they are manufactured in smaller mills. Plastic containers with recycled content are currently more expensive than virgin containers due to the relatively low prices for oil and the high costs of sorting, transporting, and processing plastic wastes.

4.7 Increasing Efficiency in the Recycling Supply Chain

Two promising solutions for alleviating logistical problems associated with purchasing secondary materials and recycled products have emerged:

(1) Greater use of rail transport; and

(2) Partnerships between companies that use recycled materials and those that collect and process them.

The opportunities and disadvantages presented by these options are discussed in the following sections.

Shipping Recyclables by Rail

Rail carriers view the recycling industry as their largest growth market for the 1990s and are aggressively developing new services to make rail transport of recycled materials an attractive option. Rail transport is most suitable for large volumes of material, so it is most effective in situations where the suppliers and manufacturers have already been able to develop economies of scale in supply. (Freight rates may also provide incentives for consolidation within the materials recovery industries.)

The rail industry offers lower freight rates than the trucking industry, but the disadvantage of longer delivery times and less frequent service, especially to small processors that are not on a regular switching schedule. A recent U.S. EPA study indicated that rates for moving steel scrap and aluminum between processors and end-users were 15 to 25 percent less than trucking fees. Rail carriers frequently target truck rates as price references, below which they begin to seriously negotiate. Rail carriers also have flexibility to offer discounted prices because most no longer must file tariffs in advance with the Interstate Commerce Commission when they establish new fares for scrap materials. (Pre-filing was mandated to eliminate discriminatory pricing for virgin versus secondary raw materials.)[12]

Closer Relations in the Secondary Materials Supply Chain

Closer relations between suppliers, other manufacturers, waste management firms, scrap recycling industries, and municipalities have the potential to address many of the problems of the current MSW recycling system. Closer relations may help:

♦ Reduce uncertainties,

♦ Increase economies of scale, and

♦ Through better communication, identify practices that would reduce costs throughout the system.

While the regulatory origins of MSW recycling programs have helped spawn an inefficient system that could benefit from partnerships, continuing regulatory uncertainty may also limit cooperation.

Companies have different attitudes toward regulatory threats. Some firms are willing to invest in new technologies and facilities to try to pre-empt legislation. Other firms try to avoid changing current business practices and fight proposed rules. The polarity of these attitudes results in inconsistent views within industry about cooperatively developing new markets for recyclables. In addition, cooperation between different links in the supply chain is also retarded by the fact that recycling regulations benefit some companies while penalizing others. As a result, relations between potential business partners might be spoiled by their differing views on future regulations.

As the impediments to efficiency of MSW recycling have been more clearly identified, companies have found that partnerships offer a potential solution. The threat of additional minimum content standards, for example, has given manufacturers an incentive to find common ground with collectors and processors. Partnerships formed to date have had several major objectives, as outlined in the following three paragraphs.

Establishing Long-Term Contracts for Secondary Materials. Waste Management Inc. has formed partnerships with Stone Container and American Can. Browning Ferris, another major waste services firm, is aligned with Wellman, the plastics processor, and New England CRInc, a company that designs and operates MRFs. Cities are entering long-term contracts to sell their recyclables to secondary materials manufacturers at rates higher than current prices in the glutted markets.

Strategically Siting Processing and Sorting Capacity. This strategy can involve building new facilities or simply installing processing equipment in sorting facilities. New England CRInc, for example, recently signed an agreement with Vitro Envases, Norte American, a Mexican glass manufacturing company. The deal designates CRInc as the preferred cullet supplier for Vitro. The two companies have agreed to coordinate transportation to improve freight prices for the materials they handle and to jointly develop glass cullet processing facilities in strategic U.S. locations.[13] AMG Resources Company, which removes the tin coating from steel cans, is placing AMG-approved cleaning and shredding equipment at MRFs so that the materials it receives from municipal programs meet its specifications.[14] Shredding the materials at sorting facilities can also reduce transportation costs.

Sharing Information on Logistics and Product Design. By sharing techniques that make their own operations more efficient, companies can improve economics at all stages of the supply chain. Such techniques include:

♦ Having consumers stomp on plastic bottles to compact them before collection.

♦ Performing more processing at MRFs to increase the density of material shipped to processors or end users.

♦ Manufacturing products that are easy to sort and process, such as by using fewer materials, screwing or snapping components together instead of welding them, and creating inks that can be easily separated from paper fibers in deinking plants.

The example below describes how companies in the plastics industry have joined together to improve the economics of recycling plastics.

4.8 Innovative Practices

This section illustrates the roles of two manufacturers in developing a supply chain for a new recycled product, high density polyethylene (HDPE) plastic detergent bottles:

(1) Procter & Gamble (P&G), an international consumer products company that was a leader in using recycled HDPE bottles; and

(2) Owens-Brockway, a glass and plastic container manufacturer that was one of the first manufacturers of plastic bottles with post-consumer HDPE plastic.

The American Plastics Council's Recycling
Cost Optimization Committee

Recycling has posed a particularly significant challenge for the plastics industry. Plastic products, especially plastic packaging, are relatively new. Plastic products comprised less than one percent of MSW by weight in 1960; by 1990 they represented about eight percent of MSW. Plastics recycling is even more fledgling -- only two percent of all plastic products and close to four percent of plastic packaging were recycled in 1990. The plastic industry has set a goal of recycling 25 percent of all plastic bottles and containers by 1995.

Features that make plastic packaging desirable for forward distribution make it expensive to recycle. Plastic packaging is an extremely durable and lightweight material. If plastic containers are not baled properly, however, they can bounce back to their original shapes. A variety of resin types with different properties are used in packaging. For most end uses the different resins must be separated into pure streams, which requires costly manual sorting. Under current conditions, the price of some types of recycled resins, especially HDPE, can be more expensive than virgin resins.

In 1992, the American Plastics Council, an industry group formed to promote plastics recycling, created a cost optimization committee to identify opportunities for reducing costs throughout the plastics supply chain. The group sought to locate leverage points where new procedures could reduce total system costs, even if they raised costs for one of the system components or players. Committee members represented virgin resin manufacturers, packaging manufacturers, packaging fillers (e.g., consumer products companies), collection companies, sorters, remanufacturers, and non-packaging users of recycled plastic resins. The results of the committee's work will be tested in pilot programs and publicized in an extensive industry education campaign.

The process of developing the new container caused both companies to become more involved in issues faced by their respective suppliers. Changes in inbound supply networks, however, were far more significant at Owens than Procter & Gamble.

P&G: Buying Recycled Content Plastic Packaging

In the mid 1980s, Procter & Gamble's consumer research department began tracking the rise in public concerns about environmental issues. The environment was a major issue for P&G in Germany, which was in the midst of a national debate over the desirability of incineration versus recycling. For the German market, P&G developed a new refillable package for its Lenor brand fabric softener that eventually became an industry standard package.

In the United States, the public was particularly concerned about the environmental impacts of plastic packaging. As a consumer of more than one million pounds per year of HDPE plastic, P&G felt that post-consumer plastics recycling had to become a reality to address their consumers'

Major P&G Milestones	
1988	*P&G introduces Spic & Span brand cleaner in a 100% recycled bottle made from post consumer PET resins.*
1989	*Tide, Cheer, and Downy bottles contain 25% post-consumer HDPE resin.*
1993	*Downy bottle are made from 100% post-consumer resin.*
1993	*Polyethylene film packaging contains 25% recycled content.*

environmental interests and help avoid legislative restrictions.
(Companies routinely recycled plastic scrap from the
manufacturing process.) P&G felt a successful recycling program
would address customer concerns about environmental quality.

P&G decided to work on two fronts: buying packaging with
post-consumer recycled content, which would in turn create a
demand for recycled resin, and working with trade groups, such
as the American Plastics Council (formerly the Council for Solid
Waste Solutions), to implement local plastics collection programs.
This study focuses on P&G's efforts to buy plastic containers with
post-consumer recycled content.

P&G's decision to use plastic containers with post-consumer
recycled content required the company to revise its approach to
purchasing packaging. Normally, P&G would not be concerned
with its bottle makers' sources of supply. At the time that P&G
decided to use recycled content, however, little plastic was being
recovered in curbside collection programs. Procter & Gamble
first met with its three major suppliers of plastic bottles and
discussed the company's need for recycled content packaging. In
addition, P&G conducted on-site interviews of plastic processors
to survey the quality and volume of materials being handled and
developed specifications for containers with recycled content.

While the decision to use post-consumer recycled content
caused P&G to become involved in developing the supply chain
for the material, the use of such containers had only minor
impacts on P&G's inbound and outbound transportation
systems. Procter and Gamble's marketing and logistics system
was designed to handle a diverse product line and batch shipping
for special promotions. Recycled content containers presented

just another variation. The production of the recycled content containers, however, created significant technical and logistical hurdles for P&G's suppliers. (See the Owens-Brockway discussion below.)

The main difference in operations from the use of recycled containers related to the introduction of the packages into the marketplace. P&G could not commit to the timing of a recycled packaging rollout in 1989. Suppliers gradually switched to produce the containers with post-consumer recycled content as their inventories of recycled resin reached adequate levels. Once a shipping district had an adequate stock of recycled containers, P&G would introduce the new packages in retail outlets. To test the performance of the new containers, the first districts selected for the rollout were the farthest from the production facilities. P&G did not notify customers of the change in containers to see if they could detect any difference. When P&G was satisfied that the containers met expectations, it revised the product label to list the percentage of recycled content in the containers.

Procter & Gamble's investment in recycled content bottles did not create any direct savings for the company. In fact, until recently recycled HDPE resin has been more expensive than virgin HDPE resin. The program, however, has earned P&G valuable recognition for its commitment to the environment. Procter & Gamble has won two presidential environmental citations, one for plastics recycling, the other for the company's entire environmental program. P&G is the only firm to have won consecutive citations.

Owens-Brockway: Making Plastic Containers with Post-Consumer Recycled Content

While Owens-Brockway is best known as a manufacturer of glass containers, the company has 30 years of experience manufacturing plastic containers and caps. In 1990, Owens' plastics division accepted a challenge from Procter & Gamble, one of its major customers, to include post-consumer recycled content in its HDPE bottles. Owens' decision was influenced by then proposed recycled content laws in California and Oregon, which the company felt would make recycled content containers an industry-wide standard. (The California and Oregon laws were enacted.)

Six months after the initial meeting with Procter & Gamble, Owens-Brockway and two of P&G's other plastic bottle suppliers unveiled their new recycled content containers in a May 1989 press conference.[15] As of early 1993, 25 percent of the plastic packaging produced by Owens contained post consumer recycled content and the company's purchases of this material represented 10 percent by weight of its total resin purchases.

In order to produce the recycled content containers, Owens had to design a new manufacturing process. The purchase of post-consumer recycled resin also significantly affected the company's inbound logistics system.

The process of producing post-consumer recycled content containers was similar to the process of designing a new container, even though the change was just in the source of the material, not the design of the package. The recycled plastic resin had two negative characteristics that prohibited use of the original single layered bottle design:

(1) **Odor**. The feedstock for the recycled HDPE was primarily plastic milk bottles and the scent of sour milk permeated the walls of the used containers. The odor persisted even after the bottles were shredded, washed, and extruded into pellets.

(2) **Color**. Variations in the color of the recycled pellets from white to grey made the color of the finished bottle difficult to control. The color variations occurred despite the use of only "naturally" colored bottles as feedstock.

During the six months between Procter & Gamble's request and the development of the new container, Owens tested different recycled content levels and production methods. Sample containers were sent to the Owens' lab and to P&G's lab to be measured against specifications. Owens initial solution to the color and odor problems involved layering the recycled resin between two thin layers of virgin resin. The company is now successfully manufacturing single layer bottles. The design and testing phase is ongoing, as customers are requesting recycled content in additional sizes of containers and new product lines.

To manufacture the layered bottles, Owens had to invest in new production equipment and retrofit existing machinery. The higher working capital costs due to increased inventories plus new machinery and modifications have accounted for all of the capital costs associated with producing the recycled content containers to date. The cost of virgin and post-consumer HDPE vary, although HDPE generally costs a few cents more per pound than virgin resin. The changes in material cost are passed through to the customers.

Owens' purchasing operation is centralized at company headquarters in Toledo, Ohio, but transportation is arranged by the material supplier. Individual shipments are released by plant personnel based on blanket orders. Owens purchases most of its virgin resin from companies in the Gulf region and transports it by rail to the company's 25 or so plants throughout the United States. The virgin resin is pumped directly from the rail cars into storage silos at the manufacturing plants. Suppliers of post-consumer recycled content, in contrast, are scattered throughout the country. They tend to be small entrepreneurial companies, although some major resin producers, such as Quantum and Union Carbide, are now entering the market. Owens purchases resin from multiple sources because no single reprocessor has been able to meet the firm's material requirements. The quantities purchased from each supplier are usually not large enough to justify bulk shipments; instead, the recycled pellets are packaged in gaylord containers and shipped by truck.

Both virgin resin and recycled resins are purchased in pellet form. The lower volumes of recycled resin shipments, however, create new storage and materials handling requirements. The recycled resin is stored in warehouses rather than silos. It must be moved with forklifts from trucks to storage to production lines. Owens already had the storage space and materials handling equipment available at its plants, however, so no capital expenditures were required. Another problem is that the gaylords and skids add to waste generation.

During the first year of the program, Owens and its suppliers were on a joint learning curve as they worked to improve the quality of the recycled resin. Initial supplies were contaminated with excessive dirt, odor, moisture, and off-color containers. Since then, Owens has developed specifications for the reclaimed materials and requires its suppliers to measure and certify that the shipments meet specific quality parameters. Because of the success of these standards, Owens no longer routinely checks incoming materials.

To ensure that the resin purchased is actually post-consumer waste, Owens conducts audits and supplier site visits. Some of its suppliers are certified as post-consumer producers by Green Cross, a national certification venture, but this certification is not an Owens requirement.

The uncertainty surrounding recycled resin supplies and the difficulties of finding adequate supplies on short notice has forced production planners to stock larger inventories and to allow for an extra week of lead time between deliveries and production. Using the recycled resin does not lengthen the manufacturing process, however. Although some plants have switched in and out of recycled container production due to changing market conditions, little new downtime is incurred in switching feedstocks because the frequent changing of colors for different bottles requires similar changes.

Key Findings

✓ Minimum content laws and supplier demands are pressuring companies to increase their purchases of both secondary materials and finished products with recycled content.

✓ Many logistical issues need to be resolved to make the material recovered from new municipal solid waste recycling programs a reliable manufacturing feedstock.

✓ Inbound supply chain logistics is most affected when recycled materials are used as inputs to manufacturing as opposed to supporting general business functions.

✓ Many companies in the metals and paper industries have purchased manufacturing scrap and some post-consumer waste, such as automobiles, for many years. The logistics of these supply chains are well established; however, their structure may be altered by competition from municipal programs and manufacturer take back systems.

✓ To reduce the uncertainty created by purchasing recycled materials from the new municipal recycling infrastructure, companies are forming closer relationships with their suppliers all the way down the line, from other manufacturers to processors to collectors to municipalities.

Endnotes

1. Robert Garino, "1992 Commodity Wrap-Up," *Scrap Processing and Recycling*, May/June 1993, pages 53-60.

---

2. *Characterization of Municipal Solid Waste in the United States: 1992 Update*, prepared for the U.S. EPA, Office of Solid Waste by Franklin Associates, July 1992, Executive Summary, page 5.

3. Ibid and Robert Garino, "1992 Commodity Wrap-Up," *Scrap Processing and Recycling*, May/June 1993.

4. Bill Gifford, "Getting Good Grease," *Garbage*, February/March 1993, page 15.

5. Robert Steuteville and Nora Goldstein, "The State of Garbage in America," *BioCycle*, May 1993, page 43.

6. Kathleen Sheehan, "Waste Age's 1991 Financial Update of the Big Seven," *Waste Age*, July 1992, page 45.

7. Institute of Scrap Recycling Industries Incorporated, Washington, DC, June 1993.

8. Bill Breen, "Is Recycling Successful?," *Garbage*, June/July 1993, pages 41-42.

9. Frank Ackerman, "Analyzing the True Costs of Packaging," *Biocycle*, April 1993, pages 68-70.

10. *Markets for Selected Postconsumer Waste Paper Grades*, Draft Final Report, prepared for U.S. EPA, Office of Solid Waste by A.T. Kearney, Inc. and Franklin Associates, Ltd., March 1991, page 4-19.

11. Ibid.

12. Steve Apotheker, "Railroading Recyclables," *Resource Recycling*, November 1992, pages 18-24.

13. *Packaging Strategies - Green 2000*, Packaging Strategies Inc., West Chester, PA, February 1993, page 3.

14. Jim Glenn, "Quality, Quality, Quality," *Biocycle*, January 1990, page 61.

15. E. Joseph Stilwell, R. Claire County, Peter W. Kopf, and Anthony M. Montrone of Arthur D. Little, Inc., *Packaging for the Environment, A Partnership for Progress*, American Management Association, New York, NY, 1991, page 200.

WASTE REDUCTION IN THE FORWARD DISTRIBUTION SYSTEM

5

5.1 Introduction

Logisticians are already familiar with many of the concepts and tactics employed by waste reduction programs. Efficient distribution systems reduce waste by striving to minimize product damage, maximize the ratio of product to package, and fully utilize the capacity of transport vehicles. Recycling, on a limited scale, is also a standard practice. Manufacturers and retailers in the grocery industry, for example, have recycled corrugated cardboard from product deliveries for years.

Now, rising disposal costs, regulatory mandates, and customer requests are providing reasons to expand and coordinate waste reduction efforts within the distribution system and the company as a whole. Pressure to reduce waste and increase recycling may also come from within. Companies are beginning to establish environmental performance goals that every division in the company is held responsible for helping the company to achieve.

In this context, waste reduction, reuse, and recycling move beyond the clearly convenient and economical practices of the past. They now involve a more comprehensive process of analyzing waste reduction options, designing new packages, and implementing new handling methods. While convenience and efficiency are still major goals of the waste reduction program, these goals are now evaluated over the distribution system as a whole, not just for a particular warehouse or manufacturing facility. In addition, regulatory compliance and environmental performance join convenience and efficiency as program goals.

This chapter describes how to implement a comprehensive waste reduction program for distribution waste. It is organized as follows:

- Section 5.2 describes how efforts to reduce, reuse, and recycle distribution waste can create value.

- Section 5.3 discusses trade-offs between waste reduction tactics.

- Section 5.4 reviews methods for reusing shipping containers and dunnage.

- Section 5.5 evaluates the use of reusable containers.

- Section 5.6 provides a step-by-step guide to establishing a recycling program for waste from distribution and possibly other areas of the company.

- Section 5.7 discusses recycling partnerships.

- Section 5.8 completes the chapter with case studies of two innovative recycling programs.

5.2 The Value of Waste Reduction for Distribution Wastes

Implementing programs to reduce, reuse, and recycle wastes from distribution and other company processes can produce tangible and intangible value. Reducing or reusing packaging lowers purchasing and disposal costs. Recycling also reduces disposal costs and has the potential to generate revenue through the sale of recyclable materials. The intangible benefits of waste reduction programs include regulatory compliance, public goodwill, and improved employee morale. These five major sources of value are described in more detail below.

Avoided Disposal Costs

Every ton of waste that is not generated or is recycled is one less ton disposed. Waste collection and disposal fees, however, may not decline in direct proportion to the reduced amount of waste generation because recyclable materials are frequently more expensive to collect than wastes. The magnitude of any savings will vary depending on local waste disposal tipping fees.

Recycling is most likely to produce savings in areas with high waste disposal tipping fees, namely the Northeast, Mid-Atlantic, West Coast, and Great Lakes areas. These areas all had average tipping fees over $20 a ton in 1990. The Northeast reported the highest fees, averaging $65 per ton. In contrast, disposal costs in Montana, Colorado, the Dakotas, and other states in the West Central region averaged $8.50 per ton. Some differences in tipping fees will decline as EPA's new standards for landfill design and operation take effect.[1] Thirty-one percent of U.S. municipal waste landfills are expected to close due to the implementation of stricter federal landfill operation and closure rules.[2]

Revenues from Selling Recyclables

The potential revenue from selling recyclables depends on distances to end-users, the type, quantity, and quality of recyclable materials, and market conditions. Scrap metal, corrugated cardboard, and high grade office paper have the greatest revenue potential of typical commercial recyclables.

> ### *Savings from Recycling*[3]
>
> Bellcore, a telecommunications consortium based in Livingston, New Jersey was able to save over $1 million by recycling its solid waste between May 1988 and April 1992. The company recycles more than 60 percent of its trash--everything from aluminum, glass, cardboard, and polystyrene to computer printer cartridges, batteries, and food scraps. Most of the savings are avoided disposal costs--tipping fees in New Jersey are among the highest in the country at $140 per ton--but the company receives some revenue for its paper.

Regulatory Compliance

Although most state recycling mandates are implemented at the municipal level and target residential waste, at least seven states require businesses to separate their waste for recycling: Connecticut, Maine, New Jersey, New York, Pennsylvania, Rhode Island and Wisconsin.[4] Businesses must also comply with disposal bans on used oil, vehicle batteries, tires, and yard waste in many states.

The pressure for firms to recycle will only increase as municipalities struggle to meet goals to recycle 25 to 70 percent of the municipal waste stream. Analysts have estimated that as currently designed, curbside recycling programs have the potential to divert, at best, nine percent of a municipality's total waste stream from landfills.[5]

Public Credibility

Companies that are working to improve their environmental performance may voluntarily adopt a comprehensive recycling program, due to recycling's popularity with the public. These efforts may improve a firm's relationship with the local communities where its facilities are located and may be helpful in advertising campaigns.

Employee Satisfaction

Corporate recycling programs can increase employee morale. People who participate in curbside recycling programs or use drop-off centers for household waste often desire to continue recycling practices at work. Many corporate recycling programs have their genesis in staff-led efforts to recycle.

5.3 Trade-offs Among Reduction, Reuse, and Recycling

Identifying new waste management practices or desirable product design features often involves making trade-offs among operational procedures, costs, and environmental impacts. It requires looking at each product or material type in the waste stream separately and testing waste reduction options with respect to feasibility and cost effectiveness. The best solution for one product may not be appropriate for another. For example, eliminating packaging entirely in favor of blankets and padded trailers may work for furniture, but would be inappropriate for a truck load of basketballs.

Reuse and Recycling

Much of the waste generated by the distribution process is packaging. The volume and design flexibility of packaging make it a natural target for waste reduction. Other waste materials include used oil, tires, and batteries. These wastes are often recycled, but, with the major exception of tire recaps, they do not easily lend themselves to reduction and reuse.

Designing a waste reduction program for packaging materials in the distribution process starts by examining how packaging is used and questioning whether new procedures or alternative packaging designs could reduce wastes. For example:

♦ Could this packaging item be used less frequently or eliminated entirely?

♦ Could the item be redesigned to incorporate waste reduction features? Desired features might include:

  ‣ Reduced material (e.g., lightweighting);
  ‣ Reusability;
  ‣ Enhanced recyclability or compostability; and
  ‣ Recycled content.

The feasibility of recycling or composting a package should be evaluated after options have been explored to reduce waste through new practices or product designs.

Since it is often difficult or impossible to design a package that simultaneously minimizes the use of material, is reusable, and can be recycled or composted, package designers and users must make trade-offs among these different goals. For example, stretch wrap, which is a reduced packaging option, is not as easy to recycle as corrugated cardboard, the packaging that it often replaces. Making reusable containers durable enough to withstand multiple trips can increase the material used in the package.

Tools such as life-cycle cost analysis can help compare packaging options by evaluating the cost and environmental impacts of each option through the manufacture, use, and eventual disposal of the item. Some of the first studies have found that the packages that use the least materials have the fewest environmental impacts. They have also concluded that the majority of impacts occur during the manufacturing stage, not the waste management or disposal stage.[6] (See the text box on pages 71-72 for a description of life-cycle analysis.) While life-cycle studies are far too time-consuming to complete for every package, several third-party organizations are beginning to compile the results of publicly available studies in reference guides. Several of these guides are listed in Chapter 11.

In general, changes in product use or design offer the best solutions from an environmental and cost standpoint because they can produce savings throughout the entire life-cycle of the product. A reusable package, for example, has the potential to save procurement, handling, transportation, and disposal costs. Recycling and/or composting, however, will mainly reduce disposal costs. Any revenues from the sale of the recyclable materials usually must off-set increased collection and handling costs for recyclables as opposed to wastes.

5.4 The Reduced Package

Forces unleashed by the deregulation of the transportation industry in the 1980s helped to shift the burden for product damage from carriers to shippers.[7] Shippers now have a greater incentive to design and use transport packaging that offers maximum product protection. Other trends, such as customer complaints about the high cost of dunnage disposal, the desire to save packaging procurement costs, and the need to maximize transportation volumes, also create pressure to minimize packaging. The challenge for distribution managers and packaging designers is to develop new packages and handling techniques that protect products while reducing materials usage. Reduced packaging achieves neither economic nor environmental goals if it leads to damaged products that must be discarded.

One of the most common packaging minimization methods involves replacing corrugated boxes with shrink wrap. Research conducted by Diana Twede at the Michigan State University found that nine out of ten companies interviewed for a study on packaging innovations were able to reduce both package purchase and disposal costs primarily by using shrink wrap with some corrugated components.[8] In addition to cost savings,

> ### The Disappearing Package
>
> *A Canadian firm, Bonar Inc. is now marketing a plastic bag made out of a styrene resin for shipping industrial resins to rubber and plastics manufacturers. The bag can be incorporated directly into the manufacturing process and becomes part of the end product. The Bonar bag replaces multi-wall paper or plastic coated paper bags.*

shrink wrap allows carriers to see the contents of the package, which offers potential product protection benefits.

The case study companies included in Twede's research commented that when employees can see the merchandise as opposed to an anonymous box, they are more likely to handle it gently.[9] Some carriers, however, view the shrink wrap and corrugated cardboard combinations as too skimpy. They say that workers are less likely to handle these so called "bikini wrapped" products carefully because the workers believe that the shippers did not care enough to package the product properly.[10]

The divergent reactions to the use of shrink wrap underscore the need for extensive communication and training of employees who handle "reduced" or reusable packages. Increased worker training can also reduce product damage and thereby reduce waste, even if the packaging is not altered. For example, special emphasis can be placed on the need to stack packages carefully, move them gently, and inspect transport containers for leaks and nails that could damage the package.

Other changes in handling practices, such as the use of more specific labels, rack systems for warehouse storage, and new stacking techniques can all reduce fiber requirements for containers.

- ◆ Specific instructions such as "Load This End First" or "Do Not Double Stack" could replace more general warnings such as "Fragile" or "Handle with Care," neither of which provides handlers with guidance on the best way to handle the package to avoid damage.

♦ In warehouses without rack systems, corrugated boxes must be designed to withstand compression in a five pallet high stack. The procurement savings from purchasing lighter weight containers may offset the cost of building rack systems for storage.

Sears: Getting Suppliers to Reduce, Reuse, and Recycle

Sears, Roebuck and Co. has teamed with its suppliers in a comprehensive source reduction and recycling program to reduce the volume of packaging for products sold at Sears by 25 percent by the end of 1994. By eliminating 1.5 million tons of shipping packaging annually and recycling much of the rest, Sears expects to save up to $5 million/year in procurement and disposal costs.

Sears was one of the first companies to implement the Council of North Eastern Governors (CONEG) Waste Reduction guidelines (see Chapter 2) by challenging its suppliers to meet specific goals and timetables for source reduction and recycled content in packaging. More than 2,300 of Sears 5,175 suppliers have agreed to participate.

The reduction in shipping packaging was facilitated, in part, by the spin-off of Sears' logistics operations in 1990. As a third-party service provider, Sears Logistics Services was able to renegotiate contracts and consolidate services. One major change was eliminating many direct shipments to retail stores by routing merchandise through distribution centers.

By shipping apparel in bulk from manufacturers to distribution centers, Sears cut the amount of cardboard packaging for apparel by 2.8 million pounds in 1992, a 60 percent reduction since 1990. Previously, about half of Sears' suppliers shipped merchandise in individual cartons directly to retail stores. Now, the merchandise is sorted, wrapped, and hung on a rack at the distribution centers before being delivered to stores. The new handling procedures have not significantly affected the labor costs at the distribution centers.

♦ Corrugated fiber requirements can be cut almost in half by switching from interlock stacking to columnar stacking of corrugated boxes in warehouses. The columns increase stack strength by as much as 45 percent if the corners of boxes are positioned directly on top of each other within a one-half inch radius. Treated tie sheets and glues are necessary to maintain the box corner alignment.[11]

5.5 Reusing Shipping Containers and Pallets

Reusable shipping containers and pallets can reduce procurement and disposal costs over the life of a product. While reusable packaging may be more expensive to purchase initially, the cost can be averaged over multiple trips. Total savings can be significant.

♦ Xerox standardized the design of its packaging and pallets to make them reusable. The new packaging is expected to avoid about 10,000 tons of waste, with annual savings of up to $15 million.

♦ IBM designed a reusable package from corrugated plastic for shipping electronic components from a U.S. plant to Mexico for part assembly and then back to an IBM plant in San Jose, California. The new package reduced landfill demand by 28,000 cubic feet annually and saved IBM a total of $1 million per year.[12]

Zytec's Reusable Shipping Containers

Zytec, a Minnesota manufacturer of power supplies for computers, recently switched from corrugated boxes to reusable containers for shipping its products to customers. The new containers reduced life-cycle costs by 25 percent or about $35,000 to $40,000 per year.

The reusable containers, which are expected to last for about four years, were 15 to 30 percent more expensive, but they reduce the need for storage space in warehouses by approximately 100 square feet and cut disposal costs at both Zytec and customers' facilities. The savings vary by the type of product and its shipping schedule. The change resulted from a suggestion by an environmentally concerned employee, who will receive a portion of the savings.

In cooperation with its customers, Zytec designed two reusable containers that complement its just-in-time delivery system:

♦ *A steel frame cart with slides and wheels that holds six 45-pound units; and*

♦ *A wooden cart that holds up to 24 lighter units.*

Neither Zytec nor its customers needed to purchase new materials handling equipment to use the new containers. When Zytec's delivery trucks reach customer docks, the carts are unloaded mechanically and taken directly to a manufacturing line. Empty containers are loaded onto the truck and returned to Zytec.

Acceptance of reusable packaging has been limited by its need for coordination and extra handling. For reusable packaging to be successful, it must offer some benefit to each person or department using it, such as reduced set-up time or disposal costs.

Setting up a reverse distribution system to pull shipping wastes back from customers is relatively simple for manufacturers that use their own delivery fleets and make frequent shipments to a limited customer base. In these situations, the wastes can simply be backhauled from deliveries, although the two flows will seldom match exactly. Companies that use contract transportation have found it more difficult to take back containers, yet they may be able to hire third parties to perform this service. Reverse distribution systems for products and packaging are discussed in detail in Chapter 6, and third-party services are discussed in Chapter 7.

> ## A New Pallet in the Grocery Industry?[13]
>
> The grocery industry is studying several options to reduce $2 billion in annual losses from product damage caused by poor quality pallets. One idea is to switch from two-way wood stringer pallets to a more durable four-way pallet. The four-way design offers:
>
> ◆ Better distribution of the load on the pallet;
>
> ◆ Greater trailer capacity utilization (22 to 26 can fit inside a trailer compared to 20 to 22 of the original pallets); and
>
> ◆ Better maneuverability (a pallet jack can load them from any direction).
>
> The four-way pallets, however, weigh 65 pounds, 15 over the proposed OSHA 50 pound weight limit. They also cost between $18 to $22 dollars compared to the $6 to $7 for stringer models.

Reusing containers does not have to involve designing new containers. Egghead Discount Software, for example, reuses regular corrugated shipping containers as many as three to four times before recycling them. The cartons are generic and are shipped between distribution centers and retail stores. None of the reused cartons are ever displayed on the selling floor. The company pays all freight charges to maintain control of its packaging materials. Workers are given the responsibility of screening the boxes for multiple shipping labels and ensuring that damaged cartons are not reused.[14]

5.6 Recycling Distribution Wastes

Distribution systems are commonly seen as mechanisms for delivering products to market. When a company embarks on a comprehensive waste recycling program, however, a different type of distribution system is needed -- one that will efficiently transport recyclables to sorters, processors, and end-users of recyclable material.

Most companies rely, at least in part, on the services of private recycling companies for collecting, processing, and marketing non-process manufacturing waste, shipping waste, and other recycled materials. The more of these functions that a waste generator performs in-house, the greater its need for logistics expertise in designing distribution systems for the material.

As described below, the process of starting a recycling program for manufacturing and distribution waste can be divided into nine steps.

Step 1: Conduct a Waste Stream Audit

Most wastes from the distribution process are potentially recyclable. Markets exist for corrugated cardboard, shrink wrap, plastic banding, polystyrene peanuts, metal and fiber drums, pallets, used oil, tires, and batteries. The limiting factors are the quantities generated and the distances to markets. Evaluating the feasibility of recycling requires gathering and analyzing information by material type on the quantity, location, and frequency of generation.

To ensure that the survey is representative, at least one year's worth of records should be examined and any substantial aberrations in waste generation rates should be investigated. Rates might rise sharply due to inventory purges or fall due to reduced production. Chances for securing a market for off-specification products or other materials generated by inventory clearance improve with advanced planning.

The waste stream audit (and the eventual recycling program) could include all of the company's divisions, including offices, food service, and manufacturing. A larger, coordinated program can achieve economies of scale in equipment purchases, service contracts, and negotiations with end markets.

Step 2: Review Waste Management Practices and Costs

A clear picture of current waste management practices and costs is necessary to estimate the financial impact of a recycling program. This baseline survey should include labor practices, where waste is collected and transported within the plant, and the time allotted to these tasks, container and compactor purchase or rental fees, and the frequency of waste collection. It is extremely important to correlate actual waste disposal amounts with waste management costs. For example, if charges are based on two weekly pickups, inspect the containers to see if they are full for each pickup, as opposed to assuming a ratio of service charges to maximum container volumes.

Step 3: Establish Recycling Goals and Financial Targets

Recycling programs can create both tangible economic value, such as reduced disposal costs and revenues from the sale of materials, and more intangible benefits, such as resource conservation and public goodwill. The relative importance of these benefits will affect the program design. Programs that place the greatest importance on earning revenues or at least breaking even on costs may need to target *fewer* materials than those that place more importance on intangible benefits. Only the materials with the highest volume, high density, and/or great intrinsic value can justify the cost of labor, equipment, and transportation to market.

Since the early 1990s, obtaining economic benefits from large-scale recycling programs has been difficult. Prices for most recycled materials have declined significantly since 1987 due to a cyclical downturn in the commodity markets and the influx of recyclables from government-mandated programs. For example, Waste Management Inc. estimates that the current market value of sorted bottles, cans and newsprint has dropped from $97 a ton in 1988 to $44 a ton in 1992.[15]

Step 4: Survey Market for Recycled Wastes

The prices offered for secondary materials and the distances to markets are critical factors to consider in designing a recycling program. Companies that are located in areas with high tipping fees and access to major ports will have the best markets for their materials. The high tipping fees increase the potential savings from avoided disposal costs, making it economical to recycle more material or to transport it greater distances. Port access is important because much of the demand for secondary materials is from overseas. Scrap metal, for example, accounts for three-quarters of all ocean bound cargo leaving the Port of New York and New Jersey. Most of it is bound for Asian countries.[16]

To evaluate potential markets for recycled materials from a particular facility, a firm should survey local manufacturers, waste management companies, scrap dealers, and product suppliers. Listings for these companies can be found in the Yellow Pages. Other information resources include state market databases, waste exchanges, and national guides and periodicals. Specific listings for many of these resources are provided in Chapter 11.

Step 5: Procure Any Needed Third-Party Support

Due to the fragmented nature of the recycling collection industry, companies with a diverse range of materials to recycle often must assume responsibility for arranging transportation and markets for some of the materials. Collection costs will frequently be high because fewer companies contract for recycling services compared to waste collection, and designing efficient recycling collection routes is difficult, especially for a diverse range of materials.

Factors to consider when evaluating the use of third-party service providers for recycling collection include the following:

Using Waste Exchanges

Waste exchanges act as matchmakers between companies with surplus products or materials and companies needing such items. They supply information on types of available products or materials, quantities, and location. Exchanges are often operated by non-profit groups and funded by state grants. They serve a limited geographic area, usually a state or region.

Approximately 15 to 25 percent of the material listed in exchanges finds a market. Materials in greatest demand include chemicals, construction debris, and shipping wastes. Matches can also be made for more esoteric materials. A Minnesota Exchange, for example, directed the dryer lint from a cloth diaper service to an art school where it is used to make paper and to a casket manufacturer that uses it for pillow stuffing. The cloth diaper company now jests that its products undergo "cradle to grave" service. Contacts for the major waste exchanges are listed in Chapter 11.

♦ **The difference in prices offered to generators of recycled material by companies collecting recyclables compared to prices paid by end-users.** Prices listed in *Recycling Times* for materials delivered to processors average 30 to 60 percent lower than prices paid by end users. The difference reflects transportation costs and some processing of material. If the processor or another entity collects the material, the differences will be even greater.

♦ **The cost of meeting manufacturer specifications.** The cost of labor, storage containers, balers, and other equipment needed to meet manufacturer specifications can be significant. (See step 7.)

◆ **Third-party access to markets.** Due to the volumes
  of material they handle, third parties may have access
  to markets unavailable to individual generators.

Step 6: Use Back-up Vendors to Respond to Market Fluctuations

Recycling markets are notoriously volatile and may require
generators of recyclable materials to switch service providers,
change the way that their material is prepared, or locate new
end-users on their own. Producing steady volumes of high
quality material can be a hedge against poor market conditions
because manufacturers avoid suppliers who send material
sporadically or material that has quality problems. For example,
the success of Mindis, a scrap recycling company, reflects its
strategy of providing attentive service and high quality recyclables
to select long-term customers. Because of its reliable, high
quality service, Mindis expects that these customers will continue
ordering from Mindis, even during periods of low demand for
secondary materials. (See Section 9.6 for more information on
the firm's recycling activities.)

Step 7: Design Collection and Separation Procedures

Collection and separation procedures for recyclables must
balance employee convenience and program cost against
potential materials revenues. Baled recyclables that are free of
contaminants and are separated by product or material type
usually receive the best price, but generating this grade of
materials requires greater investments in containers and
processing equipment (e.g., balers). In some cases,
manufacturers prefer materials to be loose or banded. This

variety of material grades and manufacturer preferences increases the importance of the market survey (see Step 4).

Making a program convenient for employees requires minimizing the amount of material separation and placing recycling containers at work stations. Participation rates increase and

Equipment Costs[17]	
Paper Baler	$16,700 to $23,400
Metals Baler	16,200 to 20,300
HDPE Granulator	8,200 to 12,500
Glass Crusher	1,700 to 4,200

Costs are for a facility with a throughput capacity of up to 10 tons/day.

contamination levels decrease when employees are asked to separate material into only a few categories. Employees also must be able to reach the recycling containers without disrupting their regular activities. Most programs solve this problem by placing containers at work stations and having maintenance staff consolidate the materials at a central location.

The number of separations and containers needed can be minimized by collecting only a few materials or collecting mixed recyclables and possibly performing a second sort after the materials are brought to a central location. The economics of baling the material can be determined by comparing the difference in transportation cost savings for baled versus unbaled materials to the operating and capital costs for the baler. Due to the labor required to operate a baler, it may be profitable to only bale some of the materials. The exhibit above provides some examples of processing equipment prices.

Step 8: Train Employees

Employee training is essential to obtaining low contamination rates and assuring high program participation. Recycling procedures should be part of new employee orientation. Employees could also be encouraged to make suggestions about how to improve the program.

Step 9: Track Program Results

Once a program is established, its effectiveness should be carefully monitored. For example, the volume or weight of each material recycled, the costs incurred, revenues received, and contamination rates should be tracked. Ideally the system would be compatible with other environmental compliance databases within the

Tracking Recycling Rates

Aagard Sanitation, a midwest hauling company, provides McDonald's Corporation with collection services for both waste and recyclables at 95 percent of the company-owned restaurants and 10 to 20 percent of the owner-operated restaurants in the Midwest. Aagard's trucks are equipped with rear axle scales so the company can give McDonald's a statement of the tonnage of waste and recyclables generated by each restaurant serviced. These figures are used to calculate an "ideal" bill for collection and disposal. Each quarter, the ideal bill is compared to the actual tonnage records and the accounts are reconciled.

company. To provide feedback to employees and sustain their interest, some firms post monthly tallies on bulletin boards or include them in employee newsletters.

Composting at McDonald's Restaurants

McDonald's Corporation is investigating the feasibility of composting up to 50 percent of its wastes, excluding packaging from takeout meals in a multi-phase project. The firm's Environmental Affairs Department first worked with Cornell University to test the compostability of packaging and food wastes under laboratory conditions. The results were encouraging, so the company performed a field test. Two weeks worth of food waste from 10 restaurants were collected and transported to a facility in Maine. After screening, the finished compost contained less than one percent plastic, an encouragingly low level, but one that needs further reduction for the compost to be marketable.

In the next phase of the project, McDonald's tested the system at a restaurant in Albany, New York. A consultant worked with the regional operations manager to design the test and train employees. In actual restaurant conditions, the contamination rate rose to two and one-half percent. McDonald's, however, believes that it can reduce this level by improving the training program, paying special attention to handling during busy periods, and changing container placement.

McDonald's plans to expand the program to include 10 restaurants in the Albany area. While it expects to break even on waste management costs, composting has the potential to generate sizable disposal cost savings if several hurdles are overcome.

♦ **Developing a method to clean the carts used to tote and store compostable wastes.** Transporting carts to the hauler's facility for cleaning is infeasible because they occupy too much truck space. On-site cleaning is also impractical because restaurants lack hoses in back and must avoid washing food residues in parking lots for fear of attracting vermin. The firm is considering using plastic liners, but they would add to the waste stream.

♦ **Developing a composting infrastructure.** Since the U.S. infrastructure for composting mixed waste is in its infancy, McDonald's is working with recycling and composting firms and other generators to develop the infrastructure. To make collection routes efficient and support facility development, more restaurants must compost their waste.

♦ **Marketing the compost product.** McDonald's views compost marketing as strictly the responsibility of the composting company. While some compost can be used in landscaping restaurants, this use will cover a small fraction of the material generated. The company's research has found a large demand only for compost certified as free of contaminants.

5.7 Recycling Partnerships

Many companies are joining recycling cooperatives or partnerships with recycling service providers. The partnerships offer waste generators increased leverage with collection service providers and end-markets. They can also reduce transportation costs by shortening the distance between generators and sorting facilities. In some cases, legislative and public pressure is causing product manufacturers and other waste generators to help develop a recycling infrastructure. Partnerships can supply these companies with needed expertise to design, test, and implement recycling programs.

By joining a cooperative, smaller companies can pool their recyclables. The greater volumes of a pool increase negotiating power with collection companies and end-markets. Companies that are located close together in a strip mall or an industrial park may even be able to share storage containers. One cooperative in Conoga Park, California extended its partnership to include purchasing finished products with recycled materials. Fifteen of the city's largest employers, land owners, and developers formed the Warner Center Association Recycling program, which has contracted with a remanufacturer and a distributor to produce and sell products made from the recyclable waste generated by its members.[18]

Waste generators are also entering joint ventures with recycling companies to provide recycling services beyond materials collection. Eastman Chemical, The Home Depot, Saturn Corporation, and the nation's largest shopping mall, The Mall of America, for example, now have recyclable materials sorting and/or processing facilities on company property that waste management companies have constructed and operate. These ventures seem to be most feasible for facilities that are exceedingly large or have access to additional sources of material, such as accepting recyclables from the general public. For example, The Home Depot's materials recovery facility (MRF) was primarily designed to reclaim construction and demolition waste from customers. Saturn's recycling service provider, in contrast, operates from within the company's Tennessee manufacturing facility to serve only Saturn. It advises Saturn on container placement for maximum material recovery, bales recyclables for shipment, and arranges transportation and markets for the material.

> ### Recycling at America's Biggest Mall[19]
>
> *The Mall of America, located just south of Minneapolis, Minnesota, has 350 stores and 4.2 million square feet of retail space. The mall hired Browning-Ferris Industries to operate the Recyclery, an in-house MRF, which tenants supply with separated cardboard, mixed paper, and other recyclables via chutes and mobile bins. Browning-Ferris also operates a retail store in the mall that distributes free information about recycling and other environmental issues and sells green products. Mall tenants enjoy a significant savings in waste disposal costs: the Recyclery charges $50/ton compared to the $95/ton at the county municipal incinerator.*

5.8 Innovative Practices

This section examines innovative recycling practices from the perspectives of a waste generator, Aveda Corporation, and a recycling service provider, Waste Management Incorporated.

♦ Aveda Corporation is a privately-owned manufacturer of natural hair and cosmetics products. It is successfully working toward a zero waste goal and has a commitment to recycling that may be unmatched for a company its size.

♦ Waste Management Inc., is the largest waste services company in the world and a leader in curbside collection service for recycling. The company has recently entered a partnership with Eastman Chemical Company to build and operate a recycling facility for waste from the Eastman plant, which also will accept waste from the surrounding community.

The case studies describe how the two recycling programs work, underscoring the different benefits to be gained from reducing and recycling in-plant wastes. For Aveda, the recycling program provides a small revenue stream and clearly demonstrates the company's environmental commitment. The partnership with Eastman furthers Waste Management's goal of supplying manufacturers with customized waste management services. In return, Eastman Chemical gains a convenient way to recycle, while improving its image in the surrounding community.

Aveda's Zero Waste Goal

Aveda Corporation manufactures natural hair and skin care products for salons. Mr. Horst Rechelbacher, known to the industry as Horst, is the founder and Chief Executive Officer of the privately-held corporation. He is an avid environmentalist and is willing to support environmental efforts that other companies avoid as too costly.

In the fall of 1991, Aveda began a process of systematizing its environmental initiatives. As part of that effort, an environmental policy statement was drafted with a goal of reducing and recycling waste to the maximum extent possible. Under Horst's direction, that goal was amended so that Aveda seeks a zero waste generation rate.

The difference between the two goals parallels the debate between goals for continuous improvement and zero defects in total quality management programs. While some argue that achieving zero defects is impossible and therefore is an unrealistic goal, others argue that quality-driven companies should never set an acceptable level for defects.

Aveda Waste Reused, Recycled, and Disposed in 1992	
Returned for repair or reuse	
pallets	39 tons
fiberboard drums	26 tons
steel drums	17 tons
plastic drums	3 tons
polystyrene peanuts	<1 ton
Recycled	
cardboard	85 tons
mixed paper	83 tons
beverage containers & off-spec packaging	22 tons
stretch wrap	5 tons
small plastic pails	<1 ton
Landfilled	
miscellaneous waste	46 tons

Aveda's zero waste goal and strong support for environmental initiatives have simplified decisions about what to recycle. Almost everything is recycled and employees focus their energies on finding the best market for the materials. Employees seldom have to justify their decisions to recycle. For example, the distribution manager explained, "I do not worry about criticism for the time or cost of environmental initiatives. They win a gold star here."

Most recycling and disposal costs, except for labor, are charged to a general corporate overhead account and are not reflected in the budgets of individual departments. Aveda plans to change this system to ensure that the cost of recycling is anticipated when products are designed and procurement decisions are made. A new accounting system can also help identify more efficient or economical recycling options.

In 1992, Aveda discarded just 46 tons of waste from its 225 person facility in Blaine, Minnesota. The Blaine facility houses corporate offices, an organic food cafeteria open to the public, product manufacturing and filling, distribution, and research and testing. The waste from these operations consists primarily of paper, packaging, and food scraps. Aveda also generates a small amount (less than 220 pounds a month) of hazardous solvent wastes from machine cleaning and medical waste from its research laboratory.

Aveda recycled and reused more than 85 percent of its waste in 1992, saving $15,000 in disposal costs, without subtracting the labor of Aveda employees to prepare and occasionally to transport recyclables. Aveda's discards of 46 tons in 1992 were 17 percent lower than the total for 1991, which is equivalent to a 29 percent decrease when adjusted for the increase in Aveda's work force between 1991 and 1992.

Recycling Procedures. All Aveda employees share responsibility for recycling. Employees from the kitchen, manufacturing, and distribution areas are responsible for bringing their recyclables to one of two storage areas in the building. In the manufacturing area, plastic containers and corrugated boxes destined for recycling are stored during the day on pallets next to filling lines. Office workers have desktop containers and empty them into area bins.

The janitorial staff empties the bins for office waste into a nine cubic yard container in the storage area, which is collected twice a week. At the end of the day, janitors weigh garbage, office paper, and beverage containers on a scale built into the floor of the manufacturing center.

Cost of Zero Waste In Practice

Year-end inventory reduction creates the greatest strain on Aveda's recycling system. In 1992, Aveda was phasing out its supply of low density polyethylene (LDPE) plastic tubes for skin care products. The distribution center manager had to arrange for recycling 100,000 unneeded containers. He contacted several vendors who said that they could recycle the containers only if the caps, which were made from a different resin, were removed. The distribution center received a quote of $5,000 to remove the caps. Since this charge was for labor rather than recycling services, it would come out of the distribution center's budget. The distribution manager contacted the Director of Environmental Affairs for assistance. The Director initially felt that this was a case where the cost of recycling outweighed the benefit. He contacted the Finance Vice President for input, who surprisingly agreed to the charge. In the end, another vendor was found to remove the caps for $1,000. After this task was completed, the containers were recycled.

The Distribution Manager oversees the recycling of mixed paper, product packaging, soft drink containers, and shipping wastes. Distribution center employees identify markets for materials and call recycling vendors for pickups when storage containers reach capacity. They also spend three to four hours a day baling cardboard, but this process is expected to change as the company plans to switch to using a compactor for recyclables and smaller roll-off containers for waste.

On collection days, someone from the distribution center helps the third-party service provider load the recyclables onto the truck and logs the units of shipping wastes collected for recycling. These items are not weighed by the maintenance staff. To cope with changing market conditions, the distribution center has formed relationships with several local vendors for each material type.

The Environmental Affairs Director oversees recycling of wastes from other areas of the building, especially when materials are transported by Aveda employees to local markets. He also assists the Distribution Manager in finding markets for difficult to recycle items.

Recycling Markets. While the majority of recyclables are collected and marketed by a waste services company, Aveda finds its own markets for less common materials. Food waste is collected twice a week from the cafeteria for a $30 per month fee and is transported to a local pig farm. Broken pallets are refurbished by a local businessman who charges $4.50 a pallet for transportation and labor. Approximately four times a year, Aveda employees travel 100 miles round trip to deliver five-gallon high density polyethylene (HDPE) and polyethylene terephalate (PET) plastic containers and pails to a Lakeville, Minnesota facility for processing. Aveda employees also take polystyrene peanuts to a local packaging store. Solvents are collected and recycled by Safety Kleen.

Reuse and Recycling

Leslie Packaging collects and recycles Aveda's shrink wrap and strapping tape through a Mobil Corporation program. By providing take back service, Mobil also won Aveda's business for new shrink wrap purchases. Mobil "closes the loop" by selling Aveda a recycled content stretch wrap for hand-held applications, which costs approximately 1 cent extra per pound compared to 100 percent virgin resin wrap.

Partnership Between Waste Management Inc. and Eastman Chemical Co.

In late 1989, Eastman Chemical Co. approached Waste Management Inc. (WMI) with a proposal to form a partnership whereby WMI would build and operate a MRF at Eastman Chemical's plastic bottle manufacturing plant in Kingsport, Tennessee. Eastman was sending most of its non-hazardous waste to a company-owned incinerator on site. Its recycling program consisted of contracting with an independent local businessman to collect corrugated cardboard stacked loose on loading docks.

Under the terms of the proposal, Eastman would lease a parcel of land for the MRF next to its 1200 acre plant and would guarantee to supply recyclables equal to 25 percent of the MRF's capacity or pay WMI the equivalent in processing fees. WMI agreed to finance the facility's $2.6 million capital cost and cover all operating costs. This plant, known as the Recycle America Tri-Cities recycling facility, opened early in 1990, eight months after the two companies signed a contract.

At the time of the MRF's construction, little residential or commercial waste was recycled in Kingsport or most of the surrounding communities. While Tennessee had a waste planning law, the State's recycling goal was not established until 1991. The goal calls for reducing waste 25 percent by 1996. The State law does not require businesses or households to recycle, instead county governments, acting alone or in regional groups, must develop programs to meet the goal.[20] By helping to establish the local recycling infrastructure, the new MRF provided significant positive public relations for Eastman.

By June 1990, WMI won a competitive bid to process recyclables collected by the city from 15,000 homes. Subsequently, WMI won a contract to offer recycling subscription services directly to individual homes. Five thousand households have signed up with WMI for this service in the area.

The new MRF is primarily a sorting facility: recyclables are sent to other companies for processing into raw materials. Equipment includes a conveyor belt/sorting line for commingled food and beverage containers, a large baler that can handle plastics, aluminum, and paper, a glass crusher, and a shredder for confidential papers.

WMI collects corrugated cardboard from Eastman's loading docks. Inside the plant, the cardboard is stored in containers that Eastman employees place near manufacturing lines.

Recycle America Tri-Cities Statistics

Capacity: 50 tons/day
Recyclables from Eastman: 15 tons/day
Inventory level: $10,000 to $12,000
Inventory turnover: weekly
Plant Size: 20,000 square feet
No. of Employees: 13
Capital costs: $2.6 million

When the containers are full, Eastman employees tow them by

tractor to a loading dock and empty them into a six cubic yard containers. WMI uses a front-end loader to transport cardboard to the MRF. Eastman, however, transports office paper and lower volume recyclables, such as mixed beverage containers from the cafeteria, banding, cellulose fiber, and off-spec PET bottles, directly to the MRF itself in rear-end loaders.

At the MRF, the non-confidential office paper and corrugated cardboard from Eastman and the newsprint from the residential recycling program are dumped on the floor next to the baler. Workers sift through the piles to remove contaminants, such as rubber bands, beverage containers, and plastic film. The office paper is then shredded and baled. Newsprint and corrugated cardboard are baled immediately.

The confidential office paper requires special handling procedures. Depending on the need for security, an Eastman employee will wait at the MRF while WMI workers shred the material.

WMI and municipal trucks serving the local residences bring glass, plastic, and metal food and beverage containers to the MRF. The beverage containers are disgorged onto the facility floor, where workers pick out obvious contaminants. Then the material is shoveled into a pit at the base of the conveyor line. The inclined conveyor pulls the materials up to waist level where workers sort them by type and, for glass, by color. The plastic and metal containers are placed onto another conveyor belt, which drops them into wheeled metal cages. A fork lift operator pushes the full cages to the baler. The glass bottles are crushed and stored in a roll-off container.

The MRF management staff meets regularly with Eastman employees to discuss quality issues. WMI provides Eastman with a report of the types and amounts of material collected from each plant location. Strategies are discussed for reducing contamination rates and adjusting collection schedules, if needed. Eastman also notifies WMI of any changes in procedures, such as a switch from metal banding to plastic banding.

The MRF manager is responsible for marketing and transporting the sorted recyclables. The manager has the option of selling materials through WMI's two partners, Paper Recycling International (a joint venture with Stone Container) and American National Can (a beverage container manufacturer). For local markets, WMI often supplies transportation. More distant users of the recyclables arrange for trailers to pick up materials at the MRF.

Key Findings

✓ Some companies are expanding their recycling programs beyond the obvious targets such as corrugated cardboard and office paper. Comprehensive programs may be motivated by legislation, rising disposal costs, and internal environmental goals.

✓ If the primary goal of the recycling program is to maximize revenues, fewer materials will be recovered than if the goal is to achieve more intangible benefits.

✓ Due to the local fragmented nature of the recycling industry, companies recovering several materials are likely to assume responsibility for arranging processing and marketing for some material themselves.

✓ Establishing broad based recycling programs is similar to creating a new product distribution system, except that the recyclables must be sent to sorters, processors, and manufacturers, not to distributors and retailers.

✓ Distribution offers excellent opportunities to reduce waste through the use of shrink wrapped packaging and reusable containers. Logisticians should have input into the design of such packaging.

✓ Life-cycle analysis estimates savings and environmental benefits from the use of recyclable, reduced, or reusable containers.

✓ Source reduction of materials offers better opportunities for savings than recycling. Reduction lowers purchase, use, and disposal costs. Recycling office and distribution wastes is most likely to offset disposal costs.

Endnotes

1. Susan Sheets and Edward Repa, *1990 Landfill Tipping Fee Survey*, National Solid Wastes Management Association, Washington, DC, 1991, page 1.

2. Edward W. Repa, "Status of State Adequacy Determinations Under Subtitle D," *Waste Age*, April 1993, page 28.

3. "Bellcore Saves $1 Million Through Recycling Program," *Business and the Environment*, May 1992, page 9.

4. *Special Report: Recycling in the States, 1990 Review*, National Solid Wastes Management Association, Washington, DC, September 1991, page 7.

5. Patrick Walsh, Wayne Pferdehirt, and Phil O'Leary, "Collection of Recyclables from Multifamily Housing and Businesses," *Waste Age*, April 1993, page 98.

6. Frank Ackerman, "Analyzing the True Costs of Packaging," *Biocycle*, April 1993, pages 68-70.

7. Diana Twede, "Factors Influencing the Reduction of Distribution Packaging Waste," Michigan State University, School of Packaging, pages 7-9.

8. Ibid, page 21.

9. Ibid, page 24.

10. Jay Gordon, "Packaging Partnerships," *Distribution*, March 1992, page 66.

11. Tom Andel, "Don't Recycle When You Can Recirculate," *Transportation and Distribution*, September 1991, page 68.

12. Allen Perry, "Source Reduction: Moving Ahead," *Proceedings: Second United States Conference on Municipal Solid Waste Management*, U.S. EPA, Office of Solid Waste, Washington, DC, June 2-5, 1992, pages 419-420.

13. James Aaron Cooke, "Block vs. Stringer: Which Pallet is Best?," *Traffic Management*, February 1993, pages 36-38.

14. E.J. Muller, "Reuse It, Don't Lose It," *Distribution*, March 1992, pages 70-71.

15. Waste Management of North America Inc., *Recycling in the 90's, A Shared Responsibility*, 1992, page 4.

16. William Rathje and Cullen Murphy, *Rubbish! The Archaeology of Garbage What Our Garbage Tell Us About Ourselves*, HarperCollins Publishers, New York, NY, page 45.

17. *Handbook: Materials Recovery Facility for Municipal Solid Waste*, U.S. EPA, Office of Research and Development, September 1991, page 2-77.

18. "California Companies Start Closed-Loop Recycling Project," *Business and the Environment*, Cutter Information Corp., June 1992, pages 9-10.

---

19. "Firms Fight the Economy," *Star Tribune*, Metro Edition, November 21, 1992, page 1D.

20. Jim Glenn, "The State of Garbage in America: Solid Waste Legislation," *Biocycle*, May 1992, page 36.

DESIGNING REVERSE DISTRIBUTION SYSTEMS FOR REUSE AND RECYCLING

6.1 Introduction

In reverse distribution systems, companies pull their products and/or packaging back from point of use to specific facilities. Logistics managers are probably most familiar with reverse distribution systems that support product recall, exchange, and repair programs. In the case of product recalls, for example, manufacturers attempt to isolate the problem production run; trace the defective lot through the forward distribution channel; pull products from shelves, warehouses, and customers; and finally consolidate the defective products at a central point for disposal. Increasingly, however, reverse distribution systems are designed to reuse or recycle shipping packaging and to a lesser extent recover products and primary packaging. This chapter focuses on reverse distribution systems for reuse and recycling, such as product take-back programs.

By establishing a reverse distribution system for reuse and recycling, companies assume responsibility for collecting, transporting, processing, and marketing recyclable or reusable materials (i.e., secondary materials). Reverse distribution systems reflect a fundamental shift in waste management responsibility from the private waste management industry and local governments toward manufacturers, distributors, and retailers. Managing reverse distribution systems for shipping wastes is likely to become a routine logistics function; and while take-back programs for other products are likely to remain relatively rare, where implemented, they will clearly present interesting opportunities for logistics personnel.

This chapter is organized as follows:

♦ Section 6.2 explores differences between the two general types of reverse distribution systems -- closed and open loop systems.

♦ Section 6.3 discusses the value of reverse distribution systems to the firms that support them.

♦ Section 6.4 provides a general guide to establishing reverse distribution systems for products and packaging.

♦ Section 6.5 profiles two industry leaders in developing reverse distribution systems: Xerox Corporation and Bristol-Myers Squibb.

6.2 Closed and Open Loop Systems

Reverse distribution systems for reuse and recycling take two forms: closed loop systems and open loop systems. In a closed loop system, companies pull back their products and either refurbish and resell or reuse them or recycle them into new products. Closed loop systems often require adjustments in product design and procurement practices, as well as reconfiguring the inbound supply chain (see Chapter 4).

In an open loop system, manufacturers assume responsibility for collecting and finding markets for their products, but do not use the recovered materials themselves. Increasingly, industry trade associations play a role in establishing open loop, product take-back systems. The box on the next page describes one example.

Closed and open loop systems differ in several fundamental ways:

- Closed loop systems are not subject to short-term fluctuations in the secondary materials market since they directly use secondary materials as production inputs. Open loop systems are subject to unpredictable swings in the price of secondary materials.

- If the recyclable or reusable materials contain any hazardous constituents, environmental liability exposure may also be a significant concern to all the parties involved in the reverse distribution system. When a manufacturer's products can create environmental liabilities, the manufacturer may establish a closed loop system to reduce its exposure to liabilities from the actions of third parties.

- Manufacturers often initiate closed loop systems to reclaim certain high-value products for economic reasons. The more common open loop systems usually represent responses to new or potential legislation. They may also represent an extension of a corporation's environmental philosophy.

Other differences between closed and open loop systems are identified in the discussion below.

Recycling Rechargeable Batteries

Minnesota and New Jersey are in the vanguard of rechargeable battery recycling. They require rechargeable batteries to be removable from products and further require battery manufacturers and, in Minnesota, product manufacturers to collect and recycle these batteries.

In 1991, the Portable Rechargeable Battery Association (PRBA) was founded to address these mandates. PRBA represents most manufacturers of nickel cadmium, scaled lead-acid (SLA) batteries, and equipment powered by these batteries (e.g., power tools, personal computers). PRBA established recycling programs in both states, which take back batteries from designated collection points, consolidate and sort them at statewide disassembly centers, and ship them to recycling facilities. PRBA had to overcome several complexities in establishing this reverse distribution system:

♦ <u>Hazardous Waste Rules</u>. Used nickel cadmium batteries are generally classified as hazardous waste when collected from commercial programs. (When collected from households, they are classified as non-hazardous.) PRBA has established separate reverse distribution systems for batteries from these two sources. Complying with hazardous waste rules greatly increases reverse distribution costs. For example, the rules limit the time that commercial take-backs can be stored prior to recycling, which affects shipment frequencies and sizes.

♦ <u>Independent Manufacturer Recycling Options</u>. Several PRBA members have established their own recycling channels. Hence, depending on the battery or product manufacturer, a consumer may have different recycling options. In Minnesota, PRBA operates a toll free phone number to provide consumers with routing options.

♦ <u>Negotiating Recycling Agreements</u>. PRBA discovered that significant economies can be gained in recycling large volumes of used batteries. Recycling vendor options, however, are limited and the terms for recycling are difficult to negotiate.

♦ <u>Coordination with Local Programs</u>. PRBA has also negotiated cost sharing arrangements with municipal and county recycling centers where recycled batteries are intercepted and separated from the municipal solid waste stream.

6.3 Creating Value in Reverse Distribution Systems

Although reverse distribution systems rarely generate short-term profits, they can create long-term value for a company in several different ways, including the following:

Reclaim Valuable Materials

The value of some products and components reclaimed from customers significantly exceeds the cost of product take-back. Typical candidates for take-back include vending machines, computers, telephone equipment, and circuit boards. Reclamation and reuse have become a standard practice for office equipment companies

> ### Mobil Chemical's Value Added Recycling Program[1]
>
> As part of Mobil Chemical's stretch wrap program, grocery distributors and other large volume customers separate, clean, dry, and bale used stretch film. Mobil picks up the used material once the customer has generated five or more bales. In order to minimize costly product contamination, Mobil has prepared training materials for program participants. The customer's savings can be significant. One East Coast grocery distributor saves $290 per roll-away container or $2,320-$2,900 per day based on a daily generation rate of eight to ten containers.

like Xerox, which reportedly saves approximately $200 million each year by remanufacturing used copiers that it pulls back from customers.[2] In addition, take-back programs for certain shipping packaging can also be profitable.

Differentiate Services and Products

Some companies design reverse distribution systems to minimize the product and packaging disposal costs incurred by their customers and also thereby differentiate their products and services. Increasingly, large merchandisers with buying power require such take-back services from suppliers. For example, The Home Depot has successfully negotiated a take-back arrangement for the space allocators that separate sheets of drywall and which an audit revealed account for approximately 10 percent of the total in store waste. This arrangement has saved The Home Depot approximately $700,000 a year in collection and disposal fees.

Comply with Existing and Future Regulations

Reverse distribution systems provide a third source of value for retailers, distributors, and manufacturers: regulatory compliance. In many states, reverse distribution systems are mandatory for selected product wastes, such as telephone books, tires, batteries, used automotive oil, and packaging, such as beverage containers. Germany has the most sweeping product take-back laws of any country, with product manufacturers, distributors, and retailers bearing most of the responsibility for recycling.

The legislative trend towards increased corporate responsibility for waste management may influence the government affairs or public relations departments of some companies to create reverse distribution networks to pre-empt potential product take-back mandates, recycled content standards, product or packaging bans, or related requirements.

Reduce Product Liability Risks

A manufacturer and the subsequent owners of a product may be liable for environmental damage created by a product years or even decades after it is produced or used. Some primary material manufacturers manage this liability risk through product take-back and recycling programs. DuPont, for example, began a film recycling program after its third-party silver and film recycler was declared a Superfund cleanup site.[3] (See Chapter 8.) Product consumers, such as the used film generators in DuPont's program welcome manufacturers' involvement in reverse distribution systems to ensure that the materials are properly handled and, if any damage nevertheless occurs, a firm with a deep pocket is available to pay for the costs.

6.4 Designing a Reverse Distribution System

Pulling back products and primary packaging for reuse and recycling requires organizing collection, consolidation, transport, processing, and remanufacturing functions into an integrated service network. Extensive education programs for channel participants and management information systems are needed to keep the reverse distribution system functioning efficiently. To date, even the largest companies have found it impractical to master all of these functions in-house. They often contract with third parties, especially for collection and transportation of the reclaimed materials. Programs to recover and reuse shipping packaging can involve fewer steps, depending on the complexity of a company's forward distribution system.

This section describes each of the major elements of a reverse distribution program. Where applicable, distinctions are noted

Product Take-back Programs for Reuse and Recycling

Product	Program Sponsor
	High Value
Automobiles	BMW of North America (pilot)
Copiers*	Xerox, Eastman Kodak
Computers*	IBM, CIS Leasing
Office Furniture	Travelers' Insurance
	Low Value
Beverage Containers*	Beverage Industry Recycling Program
Batteries	National Electrical Manufacturers Association, The Portable Battery Manufacturers Association
Film Cartridges	Kodak
Hair & Skin Care Packaging	Aveda, The Body Shop
Pallets*	Chep USA, First National Pallet Rental, National Pallet Leasing Systems
Photographic Film*	DuPont
Photographic Chemicals*	DuPont
Polystyrene Food Service Products	Dart Container, National Polystyrene Recycling Company
Polystyrene Peanuts	Polystyrene Loose Producers Council & Mail Boxes Etc..
Shipping Containers*	IBM, Egghead Discount Software, General Motors, Zytec
Shrink Wrap*	Mobil
Telephone Books*	US West Direct

* Known closed loop systems.

Note: This list is not exhaustive.

between systems for packaging and other materials, and between open and closed loop systems.

Managing the Collection Process

Two variables drive collection system design:

(1) Deciding where in the supply chain to collect the products or packages (e.g., from manufacturers, distributors, retail outlets, or households); and

(2) Selecting a collection method (e.g., using third parties in the forward distribution system, the postal service, or specialized contractors with recycling experience.)

Since private sector recycling take-back programs are relatively new in most industries, comprehensive education programs for all participants and accurate, unbiased pilot testing are essential. Even though the public strongly supports environmental initiatives, it prefers convenient programs -- MSW recycling rates dramatically increase when curbside recycling services replace drop-off centers. The take-back program should also be designed to demonstrate clear benefits, which are explained to product generators through a comprehensive education program. For example, Aveda Corporation had trouble motivating salons to participate in a take-back program for shampoo containers because the salons believed that Aveda was profiting from the program while asking them to participate for a $45 annual fee. In fact, Aveda is offering the program primarily for environmental reasons and will lose money if participation rates are high.

Targeting the Collection Program

If the take-back program is not government-mandated, program managers can choose where in the supply chain to locate their collection efforts. (Mandates often specify retail collection points.) In most cases, the further down the supply chain a product travels, the harder it is to reclaim, because volumes disperse and contaminants increase.

The simplest take-back programs are loops between two sequential links in the supply chain (e.g., between manufacturers or between manufacturers and distributors). These relationships have spawned many reverse distribution programs for manufacturing scrap and shipping waste.

Take-back programs that skip over one or more supply chain links (e.g. from retailers back to manufacturers, skipping distributors) face exponential growth in complexity. Products or packaging are dispersed over a larger geographic area and space limitations at retailers necessitate frequent collection service. Most retail maintenance areas were not designed to accommodate recycling and consequently lack space for containers, balers, and other equipment. Recyclable or reusable materials must be collected frequently from these stores, and often will be in less than full truck load quantities. The need for frequent collection is especially acute for "high-value" equipment destined for reuse. Once the lease or service contract on this equipment has expired, its value can diminish rapidly, as users may become less responsible custodians. Manufacturers that reclaim copier equipment from businesses and the producers of polystyrene peanuts both operate take-back systems that skip supply chain links.

Take-back programs that reach from manufacturers to individual consumers are the most difficult to administer. These programs often require several consolidation stages and mechanisms for sorting the desired product from other wastes. Assuming that the objective is to reclaim as much of the target material as possible (as opposed to demonstrating that a reclamation system is in place for marketing or regulatory purposes) manufacturers may create incentives to encourage consumers to return the product and retailers to serve as collection sites, if needed.

Selecting a Collection Method

Research for this study found that companies typically employ one of four types of collection methods:

(1) The forward distribution system;
(2) The U.S. Post Office and other express mail services;
(3) Established recycling companies; or
(4) Specialized transportation firms.

The most appropriate method depends on where the product is being pulled back from, the volumes collected, and physical product characteristics. While a company could design a new collection system that does not employ third parties or the company's forward distribution system, none of the companies in our research have done this. Thus, we have not included this option in our discussion.

Using the Forward Distribution System. In some cases, an existing system for distributing products to customers may be used to backhaul the products for reuse or recycling. This approach is most successful for retrieving shipping containers and pallets that travel between a small number of manufacturers and distributors on dedicated fleets. Forward distribution systems do not work well for product take-back if:

♦ The used product must be sorted or processed;

♦ The take-back system involves more than two links in the supply chain; or

♦ Third-party carriers are used for deliveries.

Most distributors lack the equipment, facilities, and experience to manage product take-backs from retail stores.

The U.S. Post Office and Other Express Mail Services. The postal service and other express mail services often can provide the best collection service for low volume wastes of limited dimensions (e.g., primary packaging or consumer batteries). The United Parcel Service (UPS) now offers an Authorized Return program where the company authorizing the take-back program can supply the used product generators with prepaid, self-addressed labels and containers. UPS collects the package during its normal delivery runs and charges generators additional fees only when the generator calls for a special collection run. The package can also be left for pick-up at a UPS express mail center. One drawback to this approach is the difficulty of regulating the flow of returned product.

Established Recycling Companies. In cases where the product targeted by the take-back program is already being recycled by the scrap industry, it may be more efficient to design the collection system to include the dealers rather than competing with them. For example, when organizing a reverse supply chain to take-back used film and X-ray plates, DuPont found that it could not economically compete with the customer service and market penetration of local silver reclaimers and brokers. Instead, DuPont worked with a limited number of dealers to design a special collection system to meet its needs. (See Chapter 8 for more discussion of DuPont's program.) The existing scrap industry is also more likely than other third-party transporters to be licensed to collect wastes such as automotive batteries, used oil, or fluorescent lamps that require special storage and handling to comply with federal or State regulations.

Specialized Transportation Firms. Companies that take-back large high value products for reuse, such as copiers, medical equipment and machine tools, typically depend on third-party transportation firms to de-install, package, and transport the items to designated consolidation and remanufacturing centers. These carriers provide special padded vehicles and handling equipment and are equipped to serve regional and national markets. In contrast, most companies in the scrap industry are local enterprises.

Locating Consolidation, Disassembly, and Remanufacturing Centers

Reverse distribution flows often require consolidation as well as disassembly, as material moves from local collection points to one or more remanufacturing centers. Supply chains that minimize the cycle time between the most costly processes and remanufacture can reduce overall supply chain costs. The most costly processes occur at different points in the reverse supply chain for high value and low value products, leading to different criteria for siting facilities.

Transport and collection costs represent the majority of total reclamation costs for low value products (e.g., packaging). To reduce transport costs, these materials should be flattened, shredded, or baled to reduce bulk prior to or soon after collection. Ideally, low value secondary materials should be consumed by local or regional manufacturers. Companies that are creating closed loop systems for these materials or are purchasing large volumes of secondary materials are building remanufacturing facilities near urban areas where most secondary materials are generated.

Disassembly costs represent the majority of total process costs for high value products such as computers and office copiers. While high value products may need consolidating after collection, disassembly centers are best located near remanufacturing facilities, to ensure:

◆ A reliable flow of components;

◆ The high quality of components; and

◆ The availability of disassembly expertise, which is often specialized and likely to correspond to original manufacture experience.

High value products can be drawn from national markets to support large, single location remanufacturing centers.

Using Third-Party Services

Third-party service providers often improve the efficiency and effectiveness of take-back programs. They may offer economies of scale in collection, consolidation, processing, and transportation because they handle recyclable and reusable materials from multiple sources. By contracting for these services, manufacturers can reserve their capital resources for ventures more closely aligned to core business practices. Chapter 7 discusses in more detail the types of third-party services available for reuse and recycling and their value to companies that initiate reverse distribution programs and other waste reduction activities.

While contracting can solve the day-to-day logistics of reverse distribution, using third parties effectively creates new management challenges. Contractors with diverse interests must be motivated to respond quickly and appropriately to changes in production schedules and customer demand. Well integrated reverse distribution systems that continually realize quality and efficiency gains from contractors may gain a significant competitive advantage.

To effectively manage third-party contractors in reverse distribution channels, a logistics manager should:

◆ Clearly define measurable objectives for overall channel performance (e.g., minimum cycle time and minimum damage in de-installation and transit);

◆ Clearly define local responsibilities in supporting overall channel objectives; and

Reuse and Recycling

♦ Maintain current and accurate decision support information.

Incentive systems are most effective when performance is measured against clearly defined standards and is directly linked to compensation.

Implementing Information Systems

Information systems are revolutionizing forward distribution systems by allowing "real time" data on retail inventories to drive manufacturers' production and delivery schedules. The same information systems (e.g., transaction data bases, inventory tracking, and inventory management systems) can be adapted to recycling and reuse systems if companies are closely linked through joint ventures or closed loop reverse distribution systems. (As discussed in Chapter 4, much of the recycling and reuse industry is too decentralized be able to implement these systems.) Sharing information about material specifications, delivery times, and supply volumes among collectors, processors, and manufacturers can integrate multiple and geographically diverse supply chain participants, thereby reducing system costs and regulating materials flow.

6.5 Innovative Practices

This section presents case studies of two leading industry reverse distribution systems:

(1) Xerox Corporation's reverse distribution and remanufacturing program for office copying equipment. Xerox's leadership in this area has helped

the company retain a cost advantage over foreign competition and has helped to spur the development of reverse distribution services in the transportation industry.

(2) Bristol-Myers Squibb's pharmaceutical product take-back program, which provides high levels of customer service in a competitive industry.

Xerox's Reverse Distribution and Remanufacturing Program

Equipment take-back and remanufacturing has been an integral part of the Xerox logistics program since the 1960s. Xerox's copiers were originally leased to customers and taken back when the leases expired. Today, customers primarily purchase machines, but Xerox has continued to offer and refine a take-back service for used machines. This reverse distribution and remanufacturing system now provides Xerox with one of its most important advantages over foreign competitors, who generally do not have take-back systems.

Xerox realizes significant cost savings by remanufacturing entire copiers and reusing specific copier components in new machines. The remanufactured equipment must meet the strict performance specifications of new equipment and is sold with the same three year warranty as completely new machines. The cost of remanufacturing machines and reusing parts, however, is a fraction of the cost of new manufactured equipment. These cost savings can be passed through to customers. For example, companies that purchase new machines receive price incentives for trading in their used equipment. Xerox takes back its own equipment as well as competitors' equipment in trade.

Reuse and Recycling

To facilitate remanufacturing, Xerox has redesigned its products over the past three decades so that basic components can perform effectively in multiple re-incarnations. Models are often built with a standard frame and interchangeable components, including motors.

How the Reverse Distribution System Works. The reverse distribution process begins when a Xerox customer takes title to a new machine. At that time, a date is set for both delivery of the new machine and removal of the old machine.

Product delivery and deinstallation are handled by Xerox's nationwide network of over 50 delivery recovery (DR) carriers. These independent businesses are trained by Xerox to deliver and install new small and mid-sized Xerox equipment, and remove, package, and consolidate all sizes of used office equipment. The carriers are integrated into the Xerox real-time information network, which disseminates detailed operating instructions.

The carrier removes the machine from a customer site by breaking it down into segments (if necessary), loading it onto a pallet (one machine or segment per pallet), and wrapping the machine and pallet in plastic film. Machines range in size from 100 pounds for desk top copiers to 1,000 pounds or more for large floor models. A computer-generated bar code with the product code and serial number is attached to the machine, and the machine is entered into Xerox's inventory management system. The pallet stays with the machine as it moves through the reverse supply chain for remanufacturing. (Xerox is currently using standard wooden pallets, but is evaluating the cost-effectiveness of switching to reusable pallets.)

The DR carriers are essentially a cottage industry of small and mid-sized companies that have developed with the Xerox reverse distribution system. The companies operate from one to six terminals that range in size from 10,000 to 40,000 square feet. The terminals are supported by three to 18 trucks, one driver and one helper per vehicle, and up to 30 warehouse and administrative staff. Most of the carriers were formerly in the household moving industry. To help these companies gain a more secure financial footing, Xerox has promoted their services to other U.S. companies in the electronics industry. In exchange, Xerox requires the carriers to protect proprietary Xerox systems and deinstallation techniques and keep Xerox customer support their top priority.

> **Minimizing Shipping Waste in the Reverse Supply Chain**
>
> *In 1992, one of Xerox's quality teams discovered through experimentation that dunnage could be significantly reduced without harm to returning equipment. The company had been instructing its DR carriers to tie down internal parts and to enclose machines in heavy corrugated material. Today Xerox directs carriers to place returning machines on pallets and secure them with shrink wrap. Sensitive internal components are still tied down but external dunnage has been reduced by 90 percent of its original volume, with millions of dollars in resulting savings.*

Xerox decides where it needs carrier service based on the following criteria:

♦ Proximity to all major customer clusters;

♦ Proximity to one of Xerox's 67 district sales offices; and

♦ Ability to complete most deliveries within one day.

Qualified companies are then selected for the network through a bidding process.

On average, each of the 50 DR carrier terminals ships two to three truckloads per week of machines to Xerox hubs. Shipments are paced by the scheduled demand for components and remanufactured machines at remanufacturing centers. Xerox's manufacturing schedule, however, is flexible and responds to ultimate consumer demand. Hence, there is significant week-to-week variability in the system.

Once used machines are pulled back to DR carrier terminals, a Xerox district sales office determines how each machine will be disposed of. Three alternatives currently exist:

Machine Characteristics	Disposition
Current Xerox model with low usage	Repair within local sales district and lease as a used model
Xerox model in demand for remanufacturing and discontinued Xerox model	Shipped to one of two Xerox Surplus Equipment Centers
Competitor's model	Sold to brokers who sell used component supplies

Most equipment follows the second path to one of Xerox's two Surplus Equipment Centers. The larger center is located in Cincinnati, Ohio and is staffed with Xerox employees. The smaller center is in Reno, Nevada and is contractor-operated.

Xerox contracts with two long-haul household moving companies to transport copiers from the DR carrier terminals to the surplus equipment centers and then to remanufacturing centers.

These trucking firms have specialized electronics divisions that are designed to serve Xerox and other electronic equipment manufacturers. (The case study of North American Van Lines in Chapter 7 examines this type of reverse distribution service.) Both of Xerox's contract long-haul carriers have dedicated air ride vans to serve Xerox exclusively. The vans have an average capacity of 20,000 lbs and are equipped with satellite tracking that connects to the Xerox inventory management network.

Once the machines reach the surplus centers, a second disposition decision is made, using 12 to 24 month forecasts of Xerox's remanufacturing material requirements. To minimize the costs of the reverse distribution process, Xerox continually tries to reduce the cycle time between product de-installation and remanufacture, thus inventories of used machines are matched as closely to remanufacturing needs as possible. Keeping this balance is complicated by the highly seasonal nature of office equipment purchases. Many customers buy new machines and trade-in their old ones at the end of the calendar year, but the used machines generally cannot be remanufactured in time to meet the same end-of-the-year product demand. Xerox handles the overflow by sending models that are not needed for remanufacturing in the United States to its subsidiaries in other countries.

Xerox Machine Characteristics	Disposition at Xerox Surplus Equipment Centers
Models currently manufactured and sold in the United States	Trans-shipped for remanufacturing at Xerox plants in Webster, New York; Aguas Calientes, Mexico; Chicago, Illinois; or Toronto, Canada
Current models in excess supply in the United States	Shipped to Xerox companies in Latin America, Canada, or Europe for remanufacture
Discontinued models that have reusable parts (handled by the Cincinnati facility only)	Completely disassembled and divided into elemental components; reusable components are shipped to one of the four Xerox remanufacturing centers; recyclable components are sold as scrap

Xerox's remanufacturing centers have traditionally been separate from facilities that assemble new machines, but the company is beginning to integrate the two processes. In 1992, Xerox reconfigured its largest manufacturing facility, located in Webster, New York, to allow new and remanufactured equipment to be produced within the same manufacturing cell. (The company groups assembly processes for different size machines in cells.) Employees were trained to both assemble new machines and make needed repairs and component upgrades to used machines. By cross-training workers within the same facility, Xerox avoids the complications of coordinating operations between separate plants and minimizes the possibility of worker layoffs when the remanufactured and new product production cycles are out of sync.

Xerox's Approach to Using Third-Party Services. Remanufacturing, reuse, and reverse distribution are core Xerox competencies. Nevertheless, the firm outsources critical services in its reverse supply chain, including its transportation services and terminal carriers. In general, Xerox believes that strategic functions, such as copier disassembly and refurbishment, should be performed by in-house personnel. Local and customer interactive functions, however, can best be performed by contractors who are conditioned and motivated to provide high quality services for Xerox.

Xerox has developed "Pay-for-Performance-Programs" that have had a dramatic effect on the quality of services delivered by its DR carriers and transporters. Xerox quality inspection teams randomly observe and score the performance of individual installation and deinstallation teams. In 1985 when the system started, scores averaged 50 percent compliance. By 1993 the average scores had reached 99.1 percent compliance. Carriers receive a bonus if they perform above standard. Xerox also requires the carrier owners to pass a substantial percentage of the quality bonuses back to their employees.

Longhaul transportation service providers are measured on their ability to meet target delivery times. The transporters are given a 15 minute window for an on-time rating; transporters who arrive before the delivery time or within the 15 minute window receive a performance bonus. Within one year of its inception, this incentive program had resulted in a 1.5 percent increase in on-time deliveries, up from 98 percent to 99.5 percent, which represents a 75 percent reduction in late deliveries.

Bristol-Myers Squibb Take-Back System

Bristol-Myers Squibb has designed a reverse distribution system for pharmaceuticals that successfully manages the product tracking requirements of several federal agencies. While the Bristol-Myers' system was crafted to ensure compliance with a unique regulatory environment, the tracking components of its system could be transferred to other take-back programs.

As a pharmaceutical company, Bristol-Myers must comply with various requirements of the Food and Drug Administration (FDA), Drug Enforcement Agency (DEA), EPA, and Department of Transportation (DOT). FDA requires all pharmaceutical companies to track product distribution and maintain a standby reverse distribution system, in the event of a product recall. As a distributor of controlled substances under the jurisdiction of DEA, Bristol-Myers must estimate its customers' normal product use rates and notify DEA of any aberrations from normal usage. This requires maintaining lists of customers, tracking product usage rates, and monitoring all take-backs from customers. In addition, some Bristol-Myers' products are classified as DOT hazardous materials and, in some cases, as EPA hazardous wastes. To comply with DOT and EPA requirements, the company must maintain records of all transportation and/or disposal of the products within its reverse distribution system.

The remainder of this case study describes the two mechanisms Bristol-Myers uses to satisfy the myriad requirements: a product tracking system and a product take-back program.

Bristol-Myers Squibb Product Tracking System. Bristol-Myers tracks all customer orders by date. This tracking system provides a foundation for the product take-back program, described below. Bristol-Myers currently tracks the distribution of the product through a semi-manual system, assigning three tickets to each pallet containing a production lot. When a pallet arrives at the distribution center, the first ticket is removed and returned to company Headquarters. The date on which the pallet arrives at the distribution center is entered into a file as the opening date for tracking the product lot. When the distribution center begins filling orders from the pallet, the second ticket is sent to Headquarters, and the date is recorded in the file. Finally, when all the product on the pallet has been used, the third ticket is sent back, and the closing date for the production lot is entered in the file.

The distribution center records the dates of customer orders in a separate file. Bristol-Myers is able to identify when a specific product was purchased by a customer by merging the customer file with the production lot file. Bristol-Myers is further automating and refining this system to directly attach the product lot information to the customer's order history.

Maintaining records of customers and products allows Bristol-Myers to identify pharmaceutical products eligible for take-back. For example, in the event of a product recall, the company is able to quickly notify customers. The take-back system is described in detail in the section below.

Bristol-Myers Squibb's Product Take-Back System. Bristol-Myers Squibb takes back its pharmaceutical products from retailers and wholesalers if:

♦ The product use dates have expired;
♦ The products are overstocked due to a specific program or legitimate reason; or
♦ The products must be recalled for health or safety reasons.

Bristol-Myers believes that its take-back system helps provide high levels of customer service in a competitive industry. This system also enables the company to maintain a "cradle-to-grave" control over the distribution of its product, mitigating liability risks from improper product use or disposal.

To initiate a product return, customers contact the Bristol-Myers' customer service group to obtain authorization for the product return and refund. If authorization is granted, customers must complete the return form provided by Bristol-Myers with the manufacturing lot code, the product expiration date, and the volume of products being returned. Customers also must complete a DEA form for controlled substances.

Customers ship the drugs with the return form via UPS, U.S. mail, or other express parcel services directly to the Bristol-

Myers' distribution center identified on the shipping label. The need for consolidation is minimal because pharmaceutical products have a high value to weight ratio. Most of the cartons returned to Bristol-Myers have a wholesale value well in excess of $1000. Bristol-Myers also prefers to avoid additional handling of its products for security reasons.

When shipments arrive at the Bristol-Myers distribution center's Returned Goods Area, one of the Area's eight full-time employees logs in the shipment, counts the returned product, and compares the count with the product return claim. Credits based on the original wholesale price are given to the wholesalers who handled the original sale. Notification of the credit is sent to the retailer at the same time. Credit is given only for products that are past their expiration dates or are being recalled. Credits for controlled substances are withheld if the shipper does not complete the DEA information. All of the information necessary to support the company's credit policy is included in Bristol-Myer's after-sale product tracking system.

Bristol-Myer measures its return product activity by the lines of information read and verified when returned products are booked at the company's product return center. In a typical month, 5,000 lines are entered into the company's computer system. At eight units per line, this translates into 40,000 individual return units per month or approximately 10,000 lbs of returned product.

At the distribution center returned products are sorted into four categories:

(1) **Restocked items.** Restocked items include those returned because they were originally shipped in excessive volume. Bristol-Myers uses strict guidelines to determine product integrity and ascertain the product's shelf life before returning it to the forward supply chain.

(2) **Items with uncertain status.** Large volume returns that arrive without explanation or authorization are set aside until sufficient information can be secured to determine whether the products can be restocked.

(3) **Items disposed of by incineration.** Inbound items are checked against a list of hazardous wastes that require incineration. Qualifying items are set aside for collection by a licensed hazardous waste transporter and delivery to an Ohio hazardous waste incinerator.

(4) **Items disposed of by landfill.** All remaining items are designated for disposal in a solid or hazardous waste landfill, depending on the type of material. These items are collected for transport and disposal by an approved company at an approved facility.

The items destined for disposal are collected once a month or every other month, depending on volumes.

Bristol-Myers is considering offering to its customers a "one box" return service managed by a third party on behalf of several pharmaceutical companies. Chemical Waste Management and Browning Ferris Incorporated, and Ballantine Associates offer this program. Under this program, pharmacists would ship return products from all participating companies to the third-party waste management services company that performs the documentation required by the individual return policies of each pharmaceutical manufacturer. Each pharmaceutical manufacturer audits the service company's compliance with documentation, handling, and disposal practices.

Key Points

✓ *Reverse distribution systems have traditionally supported product recall, repair, and exchange programs. Now they are being implemented to reuse and recycle shipping packaging and other products. These systems are often called product take-back programs.*

✓ *The two types of reverse distribution systems are closed loop systems and open loop systems. In closed loop systems, the company initiating the take-back programs uses the reclaimed material. In open loop systems, the companies originating the program find markets for the materials with other firms.*

✓ *The value of reverse distribution systems for reuse and recycling include the reclamation of valuable materials, differentiation of services and products, compliance with existing and future regulatory requirements, and the reduction of product liability risks.*

✓ *Establishing a reverse distribution system requires coordinating an integrated network and educating its participants.*

✓ *The major components of a reverse distribution system include: managing the collection process; targeting the collection program; selecting a collection method; and locating consolidation, disassembly, and remanufacturing centers.*

✓ *The use of third-party services and information management systems can improve efficiency of take-back programs.*

Endnotes

1. Perry A. Trunick, "Take Action on the Environment," *Transportation and Distribution*, May 1992, page 62.

2. *Green Products by Design: Choices for a Cleaner Environment*, Office of Technology Assessment, U.S. Government Printing Office, Washington, DC, October 1992, page 41.

3. James Aaron Cooke, "It's Not Easy Being Green! 'Reverse Logistics' Programs Put New Pressure on Logistics Managers to Recycle," *Traffic Management*, December 1992, pages 42-47.

THIRD-PARTY SERVICES

```
┌─────────┐
│         │
│    7    │
│         │
└─────────┘
```

7.1 Background

Companies with core competencies in manufacturing, merchandising, or forward distribution frequently engage the services of third parties in developing new recycling and reuse programs. The reliance on third parties has kept waste reduction staff to a minimum at many companies. Logistics professionals may find that these third-party service providers offer the best opportunity to become directly involved in managing recycling and reuse.

This chapter describes selected waste reduction services available by contract. As previous chapters have demonstrated, many waste reduction activities are logistics intensive, so most of the services described below involve transporting and consolidating reusable or recyclable products and materials. One exception, an information service that verifies environmental claims, helps provide a sound factual mooring for green products and waste reduction services.

The chapter is organized as follows:

◆ Section 7.2 discusses the potential provided by contracting with third parties.

◆ Section 7.3 summarizes the types of services available and the companies that provide them.

◆ Sections 7.4 through 7.7 present case studies of four firms that provide innovative third-party services:

    (1) North American High Value Products,

    (2) RE-SOURCE AMERICA INC.,

    (3) Chep USA, and

    (4) Scientific Certification Systems.

7.2 Reasons for Using Third-Party Services

Firms have cited a wide range of reasons for using third-party services to develop new reuse and recycling channels. The most frequently mentioned reasons include the following:

♦ **Retain focus on core business.** Developing expertise outside of a company's core business tends to diffuse its strategic focus, spread its resources too thinly, and thereby impedes its flexibility to respond to new market opportunities.

♦ **Conserve capital.** Engaging third-party services frequently includes use of significant third-party capital assets, and thereby avoids the need for large start-up capital investments.

♦ **Use best available capabilities.** Some third-party service providers work hard at being the best in their field. If companies look beyond these service leaders or attempt to develop their own solutions to reverse logistics problems, they may settle for second best solutions.

♦ **Capture economies of scale.** Significant economies of scale exist in used product collection and waste stream consolidation through established freight networks. Individual manufacturers cannot attain such economies alone, particularly in the start-up phase of a reverse logistics program.

♦ **Integrate reverse supply chain.** Third parties who routinely maintain close contact with all the participants in the reverse supply chain can often do a better job of metering reused product flow rates and managing reclaimed product quality.

In general, the use of third parties comes down to two issues: (1) strategic focus and (2) operating economics. A company may find it advantageous to set up a reverse supply chain or conduct environmental research internally, if such processes complement its strategic focus. Otherwise, third-party services are an effective way to quickly create a logistics service network and gain environmental expertise. The best test of competitive economics is the acceptance of the service in the market.

Once a company has decided to buy third-party services, it has a choice between using off-the-shelf services or proprietary third-party services that are tailored to a company's specific requirements. Off-the-shelf services offer national coverage and quick implementation. Their use and refinement, however, may be less a source of competitive advantage than the services of specialized service providers.

7.3 Types of Third-Party Services

Third-party services that are useful for managing flows of reclaimed products and materials fall into the five general categories described below.

Specialized Collection and Consolidation for High Value Products

These companies assist manufacturers in operating reverse distribution systems by furnishing equipment de-installation, consolidation, and transportation services. Manufacturers retain title to the products and provide disposition instructions.

Commercial Wastes Collection, Sorting, and Marketing

Many waste hauling companies now provide collection, storing, and marketing services for common commercial recyclables such as corrugated, office paper, and beverage containers. The national waste management companies are also beginning to merge with scrap dealers and offer more customized services such as on-site processing to large facilities. (See sections 4.2 and 4.3 for more general information on the traditional recycling industry, and sections 5.8 and 9.5 for case studies involving typical service providers, Waste Management Inc. and Mindis, an Attwoods subsidiary, respectively.)

Specialized Commercial Waste Collection, Processing, and Marketing

These companies specialize in managing large volumes of homogenous wastes or problem wastes (e.g., used oil, batteries, and tires) from small businesses and industry. They tend to be dedicated to a particular material type such as used oil, metal scrap, or paper. (See the discussion of scrap dealers in section 4.2.) Some of these companies, particularly the scrap metal dealers, focus more on sorting and processing and rarely provide collection services. In contrast, for problem wastes, collection is an important component of recovery services.

Independent Management of Reusable Packaging and Pallet Pools

The expenses of purchasing and disposing of single-use packaging have created new interest in reusable containers and dunnage. Within the grocery industry, a self-administered pallet pool has resulted in substantial savings. New independent companies that own pallets and rent them to manufacturers and distributors are having increasing success at maintaining quality.

Validation of Green Product Claims

Companies interested in producing, purchasing, or selling green products must overcome consumer skepticism about their motives, contradictory labeling laws, and differences of opinion as to preferred environmental attributes. A few U.S. companies have been formed in recent years to help green marketers by providing independent verification of environmental claims. Their methods include life-cycle analysis and comparisons of products that make environmental claims with others in their class.

The table on the next page presents examples of these types of third-party services available and their providers.

Types of Third-Party Services

Service	Examples	Selected Providers
Specialized high value product collection and consolidation	◆ De-install computers and office and medical equipment ◆ Consolidate used products into truckload quantities and ship to disassembly points	◆ North American High Value Products ◆ Other major van lines
Commercial waste collection, sorting, and marketing	◆ Handle multiple material types (paper, glass, plastic, metals) from a variety of businesses	◆ Attwoods ◆ Laidlaw ◆ Waste Management Inc. ◆ Browning-Ferris ◆ Local hauling/ recycling companies
Specialized commercial waste collection, processing, and marketing	◆ Recover used oil and solvents ◆ Salvage and compact autos ◆ Sort commercial waste paper	◆ Safety Kleen ◆ Brooklyn Salvage Corp. ◆ Paper Waste Management, Inc.
Packaging and pallet pools	◆ Operate reusable packaging system ◆ Exchange or rent pallets ◆ Recycle or reuse dunnage	◆ RE-SOURCE AMERICA INC. ◆ Chep USA ◆ Polystyrene Loose Producers Council/ Mail Boxes Etc.
Green product validation	◆ Validate recycled content, recyclability, and other environmental claims	◆ Scientific Certification Systems ◆ Green Seal

7.4 North American HVP: Customized Product Take-Back

North American High Value Products (HVP) is a $220 million business unit of North American Van Lines.[1] Since 1978, HVP has offered product take-back and de-installation services to manufacturers of mainframe computers and copiers. HVP has grown well beyond this core business to help its customers design reverse supply chains. HVP has developed the essential skills and assets to serve the product reuse and reclamation needs of its customers, particularly those with high value, high density products. These customers include manufacturers of electronic equipment, instruments, machine tools, communications equipment, office equipment, and medical equipment.

Over the years, HVP has adapted its services to market developments. For example, in the 1970s an active market emerged for used second and third generation mainframe and mini-computers. In the 1980s the business of installing and de-installing mainframe computers began to decline, while the market for used electronic and medical equipment and personal computers grew. HVP has helped several of its customers develop reverse supply chains in these markets.

Service Description

HVP's strength lies in its ability to customize a reuse and recycling network using as building blocks its trucking fleet, information systems, and international terminal network. HVP's strategy is to offer its customers a broad menu of service elements, while customizing a reverse supply chain from this menu to match specific customer needs. HVP is committed to serving specialized niches that other transport companies do not serve. To tailor solutions to specific reverse distribution problems, HVP normally uses some version of the following five-step process:

(1) Discuss the scale and scope of the logistics problem with a potential customer;

(2) Perform a field audit of key de-installation, product preparation, field disassembly, and handling requirements;

(3) Prepare a service proposal;

(4) Initiate a trial program; and

(5) Scale up the service as needed.

Examples of HVP Service Applications

Companies benefit from HVP's services in a variety of ways:

♦ They save on administrative, transportation, and information costs.

♦ The value of product recovered for resale increases when products are properly de-installed, padded, and protected for safe shipment. HVP supplies its customers with information on the anticipated versus actual condition of the recovered products.

North American Returned Product Solutions

Typical Services Offered

♦ *Receive records on returned products*
♦ *Provide cards with HVP's toll free number for customers to send to product lessees*
♦ *Arrange pick up with customer and select transport mode and carrier based on service and transit requirement and location*
♦ *Give list of products to be returned to driver and carrier*
♦ *Replace returned products*
♦ *Maintain "perpetual inventory" system that enables HVP customers to cease or commence billing to their customers*
♦ *Use triggers to predetermine disposition*
♦ *Transport product to nearest consolidation center*
♦ *Compare actual product condition with anticipated condition*
♦ *Determine how used products should be disposed (e.g., re-sold, refurbished and reused, recycled)*
♦ *Value used products using trained staff and pre-established criteria*
♦ *Allow customers to change disposition or values in real time*
♦ *Allow field personnel to access products as needed*
♦ *Send records of product disposition to customers*

Other Options

♦ *Refurbish and clean de-installation site*
♦ *Repackage products*
♦ *Manage scrap*
♦ *Store products*
♦ *Maintain physical inventories*
♦ *Meter the flow of recycled parts*
♦ *Manage small quantities of hazardous wastes*

Reuse and Recycling

♦ In addition, HVP's services can help companies comply with environmental regulations.

The following examples of HVP services illustrate its flexibility.

Specialized Equipment De-installation. HVP manages product returns for the Diagnostic Division of Miles Inc. When Miles sells new blood analyzer equipment to hospitals, labs, and clinics, it assumes responsibility for disposing of the used units. In certain jurisdictions, only the original manufacturer can dispose of this equipment. HVP removes or "de-installs" blood analyzers and related hardware from hospitals and clinics for Miles. First, a Miles technician cleans and disinfects the equipment. Next, a HVP driver removes the certifiably disinfected property from the user facility and transports it to a Miles disassembly center, where it is reclaimed, refurbished, or destroyed.

Just-In-Time Leased Equipment Take Back. The physical condition of a product often deteriorates quickly after its lease or service contract ends. Thus, just-in-time de-installation is essential to maintain the value of reusable products. HVP generally receives advance notification from its customer and schedules a de-installation to be performed soon after the termination of the equipment lease contract. Risk of equipment damage is thereby reduced and opportunities for equipment reuse or further leasing are increased.

Load Protection System. HVP has developed a load protection system for product returns called NO CRATE FREIGHT™. This system is designed to protect heavy equipment weighing up to 8,000 pounds during transfer from the original installation site, through transport consolidation at an HVP logistics center and routing to HVP's customer. NO CRATE FREIGHT™ involves several load transfer technologies:

♦ Specially designed heavy lift gates on North American vans;

♦ Padded shrouds that protect loads in transit;

♦ Special load securement systems in North American vans; and

♦ Techniques for handling special product returns.

For example, for lifting and securing heavy loads, such as machine tools, HVP has developed a "Bed Frame" load securement device that can be wheeled over the machine tools to be de-installed. The heavy equipment is then lifted into the Bed Frame and wheeled onto and secured within a North American van. In most cases, NO CRATE FREIGHT™ is substantially simpler than traditional load securing techniques. Moreover, costs are usually $300 to $400 lower per shipment.

Contract Reverse Distribution. One type of service that HVP anticipates will grow substantially is helping companies consolidate the return product stream within its terminal service network and redirecting such used products to other destinations and uses. Many companies in the office equipment, computer, and computer peripheral businesses have set up product take-back and lease termination programs.

Reuse and Recycling

HVP services for Wang Laboratories are a case in point. Wang takes back a substantial volume of used computer peripheral devices and automated office equipment from its dealer network. HVP worked with Wang Laboratories to manage return product flows from dealer locations throughout the United States and track these flows using HVP's Asset Management Product Tracking System (AMPTS). This system allowed Wang to better control assets in the field and meter their flow to the Wang disassembly point, located in HVP's Boston logistics center and jointly staffed by both companies. At that center, Wang technicians disassemble used equipment, salvage parts, and dispose of the remaining material. Some equipment is refurbished for resale.

The program has helped increase Wang's product returns for resale by 55 percent, while reducing resource requirements -- Wang reduced its Return Product Centers from 28 to four. In addition, the program linked all transactions and inventory controls through HVP's AMPTS and consequently eliminated five Wang staff positions. HVP was able to efficiently consolidate reverse product flows through its existing cargo tracking network and re-direct product flow to alternative destinations at the customer's direction.

Other Returned Product Services. For some of its customers HVP does more than package and transport equipment that is being taken back. For example, the company disassembles equipment in its logistics centers, separates scrap from reclaimed components, manages the return of usable parts to a customer-designated reclamation center, and consigns non-reusable parts to recycling centers. HVP also leases space in its logistics centers to allow customers to perform disassembly and re-consignment within the reverse supply chain. While HVP has principally focused on take backs from commercial and business sites, the company now has several pilot projects underway that take back and de-install equipment from individual residences.

Conclusions

HVP services and information systems have evolved in pace with developments in its high value product markets. HVP offers companies that are making a foray into reverse distribution a ready-made system that includes much more than transportation management. The benefits of a quick start up and a partner with extensive experience, particularly in high value product take-backs, are several. They include:

♦ Assured compliance with environmental regulations;

♦ A single invoice for multiple services with line item costs for individual services;

♦ Real time inventory, transaction, and cycle time data; and

♦ Minimum administrative and overhead cost burden.

7.5 RE-SOURCE AMERICA INC.: Packaging Recovery System

RE-SOURCE AMERICA INC. is an emerging, high growth, recovery, reuse, and recycling services company that was founded in 1990. It caters to the demand for environmentally responsible packaging, which has been growing rapidly as a result of consumer awareness, increased waste disposal costs, and new environmental packaging regulations (see Chapter 2). The company is building a national network through which it offers a patented closed-loop packaging and shipping materials reclamation service. RE-SOURCE AMERICA INC. assists with the design of resilient foam and other packaging materials and works with equipment manufacturers to orchestrate a reverse distribution system that returns the packaging from customers for reuse and/or recycling. Packaging is typically designed to be reused 10 to 50 times. RE-SOURCE AMERICA INC.'s customers include original equipment manufacturers (OEMs) of computer equipment, medical equipment, industrial instruments, and specialty chemicals and drugs (e.g., Hewlett Packard, IBM, CompuAdd Computers, Perkin Elmer, and Miles Laboratories).

Service Description

RE-SOURCE AMERICA INC.'s reverse distribution network works through 20 authorized packaging producers (APPs). These APPs are also the primary suppliers of packaging for RE-SOURCE AMERICA INC.'s clients, the OEMs. OEMs who participate in RE-SOURCE AMERICA INC.'s program direct the end-users of their equipment to return packaging materials, which would otherwise be disposed, to the relevant APP. The returned packaging materials are inspected and, depending on their condition, either recycled or refurbished and reused. The figure below compares the RE-SOURCE AMERICA INC. approach to the existing approach in which packaging is generally landfilled.

RE-SOURCE AMERICA INC. is expanding its recovery network to include company-operated Regional Recovery Centers to supplement the affiliated APPs. These centers will recover

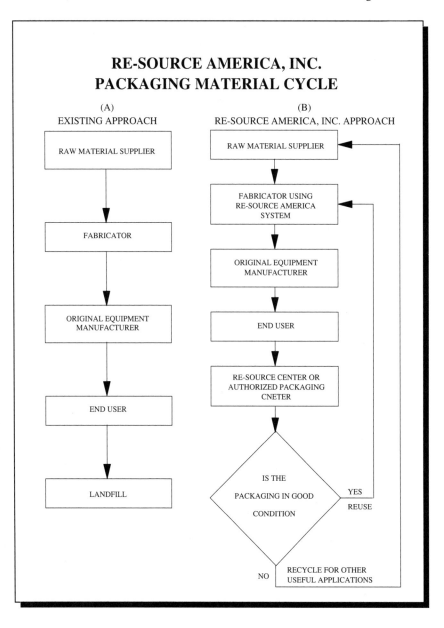

RE-SOURCE AMERICA, INC.
PACKAGING MATERIAL CYCLE

(A)
EXISTING APPROACH

(B)
RE-SOURCE AMERICA, INC. APPROACH

RAW MATERIAL SUPPLIER

RAW MATERIAL SUPPLIER

FABRICATOR

FABRICATOR USING
RE-SOURCE AMERICA
SYSTEM

ORIGINAL EQUIPMENT
MANUFACTURER

ORIGINAL EQUIPMENT
MANUFACTURER

END USER

END USER

LANDFILL

RE-SOURCE CENTER OR
AUTHORIZED PACKAGING
CNETER

IS THE
PACKAGING IN GOOD
CONDITION

YES
REUSE

NO   RECYCLE FOR OTHER
USEFUL APPLICATIONS

packaging materials from the end-user for either recycling or bulk shipment back to the relevant APP following inspection. End-users may still return packaging directly to the APP, which is generally located near the OEM. End-users also will have the option to return packaging to a Regional Recovery Center.

In the RE-SOURCE AMERICA INC. system, APPs supply specially designed, resilient packaging that can be broken down or compressed for return shipment. For example, RE-SOURCE AMERICA INC., in collaboration with Austin Foam Plastics (an APP) and its customer, CompuAdd, designed a unique, knock-down package that won a gold star, first place, in the electronics category and environmental category of the 1992 Institute of Packaging Professionals' prestigious Ameristar packaging competition. The interior corrugated piece of the box, which positions the foam cushions, folds into a small pre-addressed box for carrying the foam pieces back for re-use. The large outer box remains with the end-user to be recycled locally.

Products delivered to the end-user are accompanied by a packaging return kit consisting of a letter from the OEM to the customer, return instructions, and a return label. The end-user sends the packaging materials to the designated APP or Regional Resource Center via United Parcel Service (UPS), Roadway Package System (RPS), or the U.S. Postal Service (USPS) in the United States or Canada Poste in Canada. The limits on package length plus girth are 108 inches for USPS and 130 inches for UPS and RPS.

Packaging materials returned to authorized recovery locations are inspected against criteria established by the OEM in conjunction with the APP and RE-SOURCE AMERICA INC. The

APPs restore to original condition packaging materials in need of repair, including foam cushions, vacuum formed trays and skids, and injection molded spools. Packaging materials that pass inspection and do not need refurbishing are re-used. A stamping system is used to indicate the number of times a part has been re-used. APPs sell used parts to OEMs at a price that is approximately 25 percent lower than the price of virgin materials, thereby providing OEM's with a direct incentive to use the RE-SOURCE AMERICA INC. system.

Products Covered

RE-SOURCE AMERICA INC.'s current programs are designed principally for high value, small cube products which can be returned via parcel carriers. The economies of reuse and recycling through the RE-SOURCE AMERICA INC. System have been so successful, however, that the company is working to expand its service network to include lower valued products, larger cube products, and products shipped across international borders. For example, RE-SOURCE AMERICA INC. is working with:

- ♦ Less-than-truckload (LTL) carriers to extend its packaging material pick-up capability to include items too large for parcel carriers and large quantity shipments; and

- ♦ Ocean freight forwarders to consolidate and/or repackage products at ports on the Pacific Coast.

RE-SOURCE AMERICA INC. is also working with APPs and OEMs to develop standard packaging designs within specific product categories that increase flexibility and efficiency in packaging reuse. For example, insulated foam containers for packaging chemical and biological reagents can be produced in five sizes that could become more-or-less standard within the specialty chemical industry. Currently, however, OEMs mold their name and corporate logo into their foam packaging, which limits cross-corporate reuse.

Tailored Services

RE-SOURCE AMERICA INC. offers a rapidly broadening menu of services to OEMs which are designed to create positive environmental and economic incentives between OEMs and their customers. These services vary in their:

- ◆ **Degrees of environmental commitment.** The end-users can return all or only part of the packaging for re-use and/or recycling, thereby avoiding packaging disposal costs.

- ◆ **Degrees of end-user cost absorption.** The end-user pays for all or only a portion of the costs of returning packaging materials. RE-SOURCE AMERICA INC. has developed payment plans that range:

    - ▸ From end-user payment, with no incentive for follow on purchases from the OEM,

    - ▸ To end-user payment with follow on purchasing incentives, such as coupons, company dollars, discounts, and other promotions,

- To a prepaid program called WE CARE FARE®,"
  under which the end-user bears no direct cost for
  returning packaging materials.

WE CARE FARE® Instructions In Delivered Packages

NOTICE:

- ## PLEASE DO NOT DISPOSE OF THIS PACKAGE

- PLEASE RETURN TO RE-SOURCE AMERICA® FOR
  RE-USE AND/OR RECYCLING USING ENCLOSED
  PREPAID WE CARE FARE® LABEL

- PLEASE DO NOT ALTER INTERIOR PACKAGING

(See inside for step-by-step return instructions)

Dear Customer:

The environmentally responsible, proactive company which has
supplied you with this shipment has also provided you with the
enclosed RE-SOURCE AMERICA® Type 2000 WE CARE FARE®
prepaid pack return system.

You are the key to making this environmentally responsible
packaging system work.

Simply follow the step-by-step return instructions on the reverse
side of this sheet.

On behalf of RE-SOURCE AMERICA INC. your vendor, and the
environment, we thank you for being a part of this team effort.

Reuse and Recycling

These options allow OEMs to tailor package return services to their specific needs. The net cost to an OEM depends upon the options chosen. The benefits include the lower packaging costs, increased customer loyalty, and enhanced corporate image.

WE CARE FARE® was created after RE-SOURCE AMERICA INC. tested several alternative inducements to improve consumer response to its service. The company found that the success of the return program depends significantly on the end-user's ease of use. Early experience with customer initiated returns where the end-user paid the shipping costs, either through a personal UPS log or through the Post Office, achieved only a 10 percent return rate. Follow-up interviews indicated that internal customer authorization to incur these costs and additional paperwork posed the most significant barriers to program participation.

The WE CARE FARE®" program was developed to address these customer concerns. WE CARE FARE® labels are included in a packaging return kit, along with instructions. The end-user places recycled materials in a WE CARE FARE® box and attaches a return label. UPS, RPS, or the U.S. Postal Service picks up and/or transports the packaging to the APP, and bills RE-SOURCE AMERICA INC. for the returned packages. No paperwork burden is imposed on the end-user. An example of WE CARE FARE® instructions can be found in the box above. Typical return rates for the WE CARE FARE® program range from 50 to 70 percent.

7.6 Chep USA: Pallet Rental and Management Service

Chep USA is a company, based in Park Ridge, New Jersey that offers a nationwide pallet rental service to subscribers. Chep USA is a joint venture between GKN plc, a United Kingdom-based manufacturing and industrial services group, and Brambles Industries, Ltd., an Australia-based industrial services group. Chep operates pallet pools in 11 countries outside the United States: Australia, Belgium, Canada, France, Germany, Great Britain, Holland, Ireland, New Zealand, Spain, and South Africa, and circulates more than 35 million pallets. In the United States, Chep serves 48 states and has regional centers in Atlanta, Chicago, Los Angeles, and Parsippany, New Jersey. Chep USA began operating in 1990 with an initial capitalization of $85 million. The company rents high quality pallets and controls their distribution through approximately 150 pallet depots scattered across the United States.

Chep primarily serves the grocery industry. Over 1,700 distribution centers run by distributors in the grocery industry have signed up with Chep. According to Chep, these distributors account for the majority of distribution centers in terms of volume.[2] Chep serves grocery manufacturers and distributors, mass merchandisers, warehouse clubs, and discount drugstores. Between 80 and 85 percent of all shipments in these industry segments take place on pallets.

Several other companies, such as First National Pallet Rental and National Pallet Leasing Systems (NPLS), offer pallet rental services to other industries. NPLS, which is the oldest third-party pallet management system in the United States, serves customers primarily in the hard goods retail industry (e.g., Sears).

Service Description

Under the traditional pallet exchange system, motor carriers who move food and consumer products from manufacturers to retail distributors are responsible for returning as many pallets as they accept when they pick up a load. This requirement implies that motor carriers have to make extra trips, frequently covering long distances, for the sole purpose of returning pallets. In addition, under this pallet exchange system, motor carriers have no incentive to handle pallets carefully. Consequently, pallets are frequently broken or in poor condition.

Chep has developed a system that relieves carriers from the obligation of taking back pallets and ensures the availability of high quality pallets in adequate quantities. Chep supplies pallets to manufacturing plants in full truckloads to satisfy production and distribution requirements. The manufacturer can ship Chep pallets to any customer, (i.e., distributor), who also participates in the Chep program. The distributor can use the

> ### Chep Pallet Specifications
>
> *Chep USA's standard 48"x40" quality pallets are designed to carry 2,800 pounds. The introduction of the Chep "Four-Way" entry pallet represents a major improvement in unit load technology. The Chep Four-Way offers 87 percent top and 55 percent bottom deck coverage. It allows full four-way entry for both fork lift trucks and hand pallet jacks. (See illustration of a four-way entry pallet below.) Both types of Chep USA pallets are painted blue and carry the Chep name and logo on the side for easy identification.*

pallets free of charge, subject to certain conditions, such as their timely return. The distributer is responsible for returning the pallets to a local Chep pallet depot. Chep maintains the pool of pallets, moving them around as needed to meet demand. A Chep service team assists manufacturers and distributors in tracking pallets. Chep pallets are designed similarly to the newer, block pallets that allow four-way entry for fork lift trucks and hand pallet jacks.

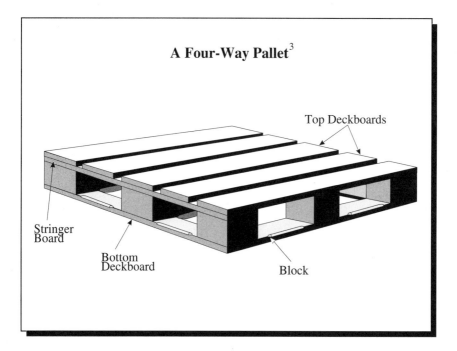

A Four-Way Pallet[3]

Top Deckboards

Stringer Board

Bottom Deckboard

Block

Market acceptance of the Chep USA service has been good and the overall service network continues to grow. Some motor carriers have stimulated market acceptance by reducing rates to Chep users.

Benefits of a Third-Party Managed Pallet Pool

The benefits of a quality third-party managed pallet pool accrue to manufacturers, distributors, and carriers. These benefits derive from the economies of scale and efficiencies of consolidating an industry's shared problems in the hands of a third party with the necessary capital, management focus, and experience to resolve them.

- ◆ A vendor delivering products on Chep pallets to a participating distributor is relieved of the operational and administrative difficulties of the traditional pallet exchange program.

- ◆ Disputes between shippers, receivers, and carriers are reduced since reciprocal obligations under a pallet exchange program are replaced with contractual obligations to Chep that are closely monitored and controlled.

- ◆ Chep maintains the pallets and supplies only high quality pallets. As a result, the quality of pallets in circulation has improved significantly and less loss and damage is incurred because of faulty pallets.

- ◆ Truckers incur lower costs in obtaining and returning pallets prior to picking up loads.

- ◆ Chep balances the pool and repositions pallets from depots where there is an excess supply of pallets to depots where they are needed.

♦ Finally, from an environmental viewpoint, the service extends the economic life of pallets and, therefore, less lumber will be needed to build and restore pallets.

A study commissioned by the Pallet Subcommittee of the Joint Industry Container Committee and sponsored jointly by the Food Marketing Institute, the Grocery Manufacturers of America, and the National Wholesale Grocers Association found that the food industry could save as much as $892 million by using third-party services to manage pallets. These savings would result from avoiding costs associated with losses in pallet exchange, searching for good pallets, and workers' compensation claims due to injuries caused by bad pallets.[4]

7.7 SCS: Verification of Environmental Claims

Scientific Certification Systems (SCS) is an Oakland, California company that was started in 1989 to verify the environmental claims of products and production and distribution processes for manufacturers and major retailers. Green marketing claims are difficult to differentiate and even more difficult to verify. SCS is pushing the frontier of green marketing by providing a rigorous methodology for comparing the life-cycle environmental burdens associated with products and packaging.

SCS attempts to ensure independent and unbiased objectivity by scrupulously avoiding any potential conflicts of interest. For example, the company generates all of its revenue on a fee-for-service basis. It does not license its corporate emblem or any of its environmental labels. Companies who use its services understand in advance that hiring SCS to verify product or process claims does not guarantee the outcome of the company's certification study.

Service Description

The SCS certification and environmental review services include:

♦ Environmental claims certification;
♦ An environmental report card; and
♦ The PACE program.

Each of these services is described below.

Environmental Claims Certification Program. Some retailers have attempted to serve their customers by identifying environmentally friendly products, but they lacked accurate factual information with which to compare products. SCS independently verifies the accuracy of environmental claims made by product manufacturers and certifies that these claims meet responsible green marketing guidelines. SCS has audited and certified environmental claims for 150 companies on more than 1,000 products or product characteristics, as well as on material inputs to manufacturing processes, such as glass, steel, paperboard, aluminum, and plastics. SCS has certified single attribute claims for the following products:

Claim	**Product(s)**
Recycled content	Plastic, paper, steel, glass products and packaging
Biodegradable formulations	Soaps, cleaners, detergents

Energy efficiency	Lighting systems
Water efficiency	Showerheads
Volatile organic compounds	Paints

After reviewing a product, SCS issues a certificate and prepares a label that states the specific claim(s).

Environmental Report Card. SCS has developed a second generation of environmental labeling called the Environmental Report Card. The Report Card summarizes the life-cycle environmental burdens imposed by a specific product and its packaging. It describes natural resource depletion, energy use, emissions released into the air and water, and solid waste generation. The objective of the report card is to present consumers with multi-faceted, yet easily understandable information about the environmental consequences of a product.

For example, in 1992, SCS conducted a life-cycle study of Wellman Inc's plastic recycling operations. SCS calculated that in a little over two years, Wellman saved the equivalent of 1.3 million barrels of oil, eliminated 240,000 tons of solid waste, and reduced carbon dioxide emissions by 730,000 tons. SCS documented environmental savings in virtually every environmental category. This independent assessment has encouraged Wellman to launch innovative efforts to find new markets for recycled material and has also led to special recognition from the United Nations Environmental Programme. The Environmental Report card for Wellman's Fortrel® EcoSpun™ fiber made from 100 percent recycled post-consumer polyethylene terephalate (PET) is shown below. Environmental report cards are distributed with the product at the point of

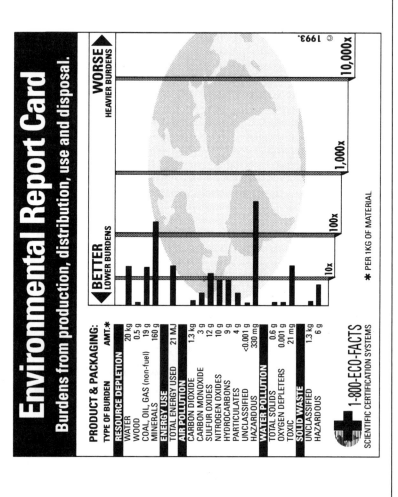

Environmental Report Card

Burdens from production, distribution, use and disposal.

PRODUCT & PACKAGING:

TYPE OF BURDEN	AMT.*
RESOURCE DEPLETION	
WATER	20 kg
WOOD	0.5 g
COAL, OIL, GAS (non-fuel)	19 g
MINERALS	160 g
ENERGY USE	
TOTAL ENERGY USED	21 MJ
AIR POLLUTION	
CARBON DIOXIDE	1.3 kg
CARBON MONOXIDE	3 g
SULFUR OXIDES	12 g
NITROGEN OXIDES	10 g
HYDROCARBONS	9 g
PARTICULATES	4 g
UNCLASSIFIED	<0.001 g
HAZARDOUS	330 mg
WATER POLLUTION	
TOTAL SOLIDS	0.6 g
OXYGEN DEPLETERS	0.001 g
TOXIC	21 mg
SOLID WASTE	
UNCLASSIFIED	1.3 kg
HAZARDOUS	6 g

▼**BETTER**
LOWER BURDENS

WORSE▲
HEAVIER BURDENS

10x   100x   1,000x   10,000x

© 1993.

✚ 1-800-ECO-FACTS
SCIENTIFIC CERTIFICATION SYSTEMS

* PER 1KG OF MATERIAL

purchase, attached to the product packaging, or placed as a hanging tag at the product display.

SCS has also worked with several retailers to develop consumer information programs that complement the Environmental Report card program.

PACE Program. As concern for the environment grows, state and federal regulations require procurement agencies to give price preferences to products meeting specified environmental criteria. In response, SCS has developed the Procurement Awards Claims Evaluation (PACE) program. The PACE program is designed to assist procurement officials by verifying environmental claims made by bidders. SCS has developed an extensive database on industrial environmental performance standards and achievements. It also has developed uniform verification methods that complement various contract bidding procedures.

PACE verification can be required as a prerequisite prior to submitting a bid or as a verification procedure to validate claims made by the successful bidder. Typically, PACE enables procurement managers to gather extensive environmental information on sourcing options rapidly, modify procurement specifications, or revise procurement policy to reward bidders whose operations result in quantifiable environmental and economic savings. The program is intended to furnish objective and standardized measures of environmental performance and recognize suppliers who have improved the environmental quality of their products. Further, claims that are verified through PACE for one contract can be used by bid applicants on other contracts.

Key Findings

✓ *Manufacturers, merchandisers, and other firms may engage third-party services for new reuse and recycling channels to:*

  ‣ *Retain focus on their core business;*
  ‣ *Remain flexible in adapting to market changes;*
  ‣ *Minimize capital exposure;*
  ‣ *Ensure use of best available capabilities;*
  ‣ *Capture economies of scale; and*
  ‣ *Better integrate reverse distribution systems.*

✓ *Third-party reuse and recycling services include:*

  ‣ *Specialized collection and consolidation of high value goods;*
  ‣ *General commercial waste collection, sorting, and marketing;*
  ‣ *Specialized commercial waste collection, processing, and marketing;*
  ‣ *Independent management of reusable packaging and pallet pools; and*
  ‣ *Green marketing verification services.*

✓ *In response to growing demand, North American High Value Products, RE-SOURCE AMERICA INC. and Chep USA have developed specialized services for taking back reusable and recyclable materials, while Scientific Certification Systems has developed a number of certification and environmental review services. These services are designed to be flexible and can be tailored to the needs of individual customers.*

✓ *The benefits of third-party services include financial savings (e.g., increased product recovery for resale, cheaper packaging, reduced waste disposal costs), better customer relations, and enhanced corporate image.*

Endnotes

1. As of January 1993, Norfolk Southern, the parent company of North American Van Lines, reorganized the HVP division. Customized Logistics Services was formed from all the different logistics activities of North American Van Lines and has the responsibility for all logistics activities of North American Van Lines.

2. Tom Andel, "Pallets Take New Directions," *Transportation and Distribution*, January 1992, page 34.

3. James Aaron Cooke, "Block vs. Stringer: Which Pallet is Best?," *Traffic Management*, February, 1993, p. 36.

4. Tom Andel, "Pallets Take New Directions," *Transportation and Distribution*, page 34.

CASE STUDY: E.I. DU PONT DE NEMOURS AND COMPANY INC.

8

8.1 Introduction

E.I. du Pont de Nemours and Company Inc. (DuPont) is the largest diversified chemical manufacturer in the United States and one of the largest global chemical producers. In 1992, DuPont had sales of about $38 billion.[1] The corporation has five principal business segments:

(1) Industrial chemicals (organic and inorganic);
(2) Fibers (e.g., Dacron, Lycra, Orlon);
(3) Polymers (e.g., nylon resins, acetyl resins, Teflon);
(4) Petroleum (Conoco); and
(5) Coal (Consolidated Coal Company).

In addition to these five segments, the company operates various other businesses such as agricultural chemicals, pharmaceuticals, electronics, imaging systems, and sporting goods. DuPont competes with large integrated chemical companies, such as Dow Chemical, BASF, Hercules, Hoechst, Monsanto, and Rhone-Poulenc, who also have a global market reach, as well as with smaller specialized chemical companies.

DuPont has relied heavily on research and development to maintain a competitive edge within the chemical industry. New product and new process developments are the principal strategic drivers in most of the consumer products and materials markets in which DuPont competes. Over the past 10 years, the company has invested over one billion dollars in research and development. Its investments have generated a stream of new intermediate materials used in fabricating many consumer products. DuPont's proprietary products include Antron, Dacron, Kevlar, Lucite, Lycra, Mylar, Orlon, and Teflon.

Increasingly, environmental issues have assumed strategic importance in the chemical industry, and DuPont has earned a position of industry leadership by improving its internal environmental practices and developing new environmentally beneficial services and products. DuPont has reduced its emission and effluent levels by 60 percent over five years. By 1995, it will have completely phased out production of chlorofluorocarbon (CFC), an ozone-depleting substance. As noted in the case study that follows, DuPont has become an industry leader in developing product take-back services and designing recyclable products to meet the technical and economic needs of its customers.

The case study is organized in the following sections:

♦ Section 8.2 summarizes the evolution of DuPont's reverse distribution program;

♦ Section 8.3 shows how DuPont has used value analysis to plan reverse distribution programs;

♦ Sections 8.4 and 8.5 describe two DuPont reverse distribution programs: film recovery and recycled photo chemicals (photo fixer and developer); and

♦ Finally, section 8.6 reviews the process of reverse distribution program development within DuPont.

8.2 Evolution of DuPont's Reverse Distribution Program

DuPont has been committed to creating value from recycled materials since the early 1980s. Most of DuPont's reverse distribution programs were initiated to support internal company operations. They were founded because of a desire to perform critical tasks in-house and avoid the excessive costs and risks of relying on third parties to perform these tasks. The primary incentive was process cost reduction through material recovery. DuPont found that technologies to reuse waste materials improved its production economics and stimulated the development of new materials.

The risk of environmental liability further underscored the importance of reuse technologies at DuPont. For example, in the early 1980s DuPont used the services of a third-party processor to reclaim silver from film. Although silver compounds are not hazardous in the trace concentrations that the processor received from its customers, including DuPont, the processes used to extract silver created hazardous by-products. The processor's apparent failure to properly manage these by-products caused extensive environmental damage. The facility became a federal Superfund cleanup site and all of the processor's customers became strictly liable for the cleanup costs under the federal Comprehensive Environmental Response, Compensation, and Liability Act, or Superfund (42 U.S.C. §§9601 to 9675). To avoid such liability in the future, DuPont established a silver recovery program.

Gradually, DuPont discovered that its customers also had unmet needs for material recovery, stemming partly from the potential liability they faced for environmental damages caused by mismanagement of product waste. DuPont could eliminate this risk of liability facing its customers by recycling hazardous materials. DuPont's recycling services (e.g., spent photo chemicals recycling) essentially create new products; the prior materials and associated liability risks cease to exist. As the generator, DuPont assumes any liability for these new products, and the original generators' liability terminates. DuPont has found that breaking the product liability chain for hazardous materials can be a significant source of value to its customers.

In addition, DuPont sells its expert knowledge on environmental compliance to small businesses. The company has set up an Environmental Consulting Services group that analyzes waste stream characteristics, identifies potential waste management options, audits environmental compliance, and diagnoses hidden environmental liabilities.

In the mid 1980s, DuPont began to expand the application of its proprietary polymer re-engineering technologies that reduce complex polymers into chemical building blocks, which can be reused in chemical processes. Through this expansion, the company created several new markets for used plastics products. In 1989, DuPont publicly espoused a strategy that elevated its molecular re-engineering capabilities to the level of a "core" competency. Since then, DuPont has applied these capabilities to diverse markets as part of its overall corporate strategy.

Before DuPont sells a product into a forward supply chain, the company assesses the potential liability over the product's entire life-cycle. In essence DuPont views a product as having a corporate liability lifespan of 20 to 30 years, during which it should be handled with "best" available technologies. Today,

DuPont routinely develops recycling and reuse technologies that complement new primary products. This strategy allows the company to minimize future liabilities associated with these products.

While DuPont has been enhancing its capabilities to re-process increasingly complex materials, the regulatory climate has been changing. For participants in multi-process forward supply chains (e.g., material manufacturers, product manufacturers, end-users), federal and state laws have increased the liability for environmental cleanup costs and correspondingly increased the value of responsible reuse, recycling, and other reverse distribution practices. The Federal Government, states, and local governments have established a diverse, complex, and broad range of new environmental requirements that both limit and create opportunities for reverse distribution programs. The lack of uniform national standards requires firms such as DuPont to tailor their materials recovery programs to regional or local standards.

DuPont attempts to create reverse distribution chains that intercept used material supplies at their first accessible points. DuPont sells raw material products to other manufacturers that produce films, fibers, and engineering resins. These customers sell their products to other manufacturers who produce consumer products (e.g., video cassettes and auto battery cases) that contain DuPont polymers and other materials. The complexity of sorting and separating these materials increases from primary to secondary to tertiary consumers and finally to post-consumer waste. The quality of the waste stream and the predictability of its flow decline at each step in the process, while the complexity of the material increases. Materials such as plastic, for example, are easier to recycle if they are a homogenous industrial scrap instead of part of a composite waste stream. While DuPont is developing advanced technologies to sort complex plastic waste streams, including composites, the opportunities to create economic value in applying these advanced processes are still limited.

8.3 Value Analysis in Planning Reverse Distribution

Before starting a new program, DuPont analyzes the value of each reverse distribution chain from the perspective of both customers and alternative material sourcing within DuPont. In a typical analysis, DuPont managers determine the value potential for each product and by-product at each link in the supply chain, including original manufacture, retail sales, collection, refining, reuse, and/or sales of recycled processed products. The value of services and recycled products that DuPont may consider offering are measured against the best alternative currently available. At one stage of the reverse supply chain, the best alternative may be virgin materials; at other stages, it may be other recycled material or purchased waste disposal services.

DuPont enters a particular reverse distribution chain only when:

- ◆ It can create value, that is, when its costs are less than the best alternative; and, more importantly

- ◆ It can sustain value, by virtue of:

  - ‣ Its position in complementary forward supply chains, or

▸ Its unique competencies in recycling processes, transportation, or product reuse.

Collection and transportation costs in a reverse chain typically range between 30 and 50 percent of total recycled product cost and are therefore an important determinant of program feasibility.

As part of its value analysis, DuPont typically assesses the disposal alternatives of the used materials collected using the following hierarchical analysis:

♦ At the top of DuPont's value hierarchy is <u>reuse</u> of the original material. Thus, DuPont first determines whether reusing the product is economically feasible.

♦ Next are various methods for profitably <u>recycling</u> different components or all of the product. This option is preferred for recycled polymers derived from film base.

♦ Third is <u>energy recovery</u>. The value of the energy recovered may or may not exceed the cost of energy recovery. For example, DuPont attempts to balance supply and demand for recycled polymer derived from used film so that recycling is maximized and energy recovery is minimal.

♦ The last alternative is <u>landfilling</u>, which has a negative value.

When engineering reverse distribution chains, DuPont seeks partners with complementary competencies within the chain. DuPont's own core competencies are in high-technology molecular re-engineering (e.g., plastics recycling). DuPont typically looks to joint venture partners, agents, contract vendors, and affiliated service companies to provide customer service, collection, consolidation, and transportation. DuPont also attempts to leverage existing corporate assets when developing new reverse distribution channels, such as its tank truck fleet, rail tank car fleet, waste water treatment and energy recovery facilities, and chemical processing plants.

8.4 Film Recovery Program

This section details the organization and operation of one of DuPont's reverse distribution programs: the Film Recovery Program, which was developed initially to address internal corporate needs, but subsequently grew into a $25 million business unit within three years. Section 8.5 describes a second reverse distribution program: DuPont's Recycled Film Fixer and Recycled Developer Program, which is a spin-off of the Film Recovery Program.

Both programs are largely closed loop reverse distribution systems, where DuPont recovers its used products and, in the case of film, other company's products for reclamation and recycling and sells the resulting new products. The reverse distribution chain that currently supports these programs has a customer base of 2,500 generators in the United States, Canada, and Mexico; 30 dedicated DuPont employees; six dedicated processing, recovery, and transshipment sites operated under contract to DuPont; and 12 DuPont-owned facilities which are shared with other business units.

DuPont's Film Recovery Program targets three markets: offset printing, medical services, and electronics. Other DuPont strategic business units sell film products and photographic chemicals in these markets. Companies in these markets face increasingly stringent, complex, and costly requirements concerning the disposal of used film, developer, and fixer, as the following example illustrates.

Until recently, hospitals would retain X-ray films in their archives until the records were no longer useful, typically five to six years, and would then sell the films to local collectors who would extract and sell the silver content. In 1991, however, many hospitals and other generators of used film were compelled to re-examine their used film management practices after the U.S. Environmental Protection Agency (EPA) identified two large silver film recovery operations as Superfund hazardous waste cleanup sites. Inadequately stored hazardous chemicals at these sites in New Jersey and Tennessee reportedly leaked into soil and ground water and threatened the health of surrounding communities.

To pay for the cleanup, EPA sought contributions, not only from the site owners, but also from the hospitals, printers, radiographers, other generators of used film, and other parties that generated or handled hazardous substances released at the site. Under the federal Superfund statute, the site owners as well as other parties involved in generating, managing, or arranging for the delivery (e.g., film collectors, brokers, and freight carriers) of the hazardous substances released at the site are strictly liable for the cleanup costs and natural resource damages. Under the Superfund liability standard, each liable party may, in principle, be held responsible for all of the costs.

As a result of this heightened awareness of the risks of environmental liability, generators of used film have become increasingly careful about the treatment and ultimate disposal of their used film. Previously, hospitals, printers, and others transferred their used film to collectors with little knowledge about where and how the film was eventually processed. In many instances, film was processed in ways that created significant environmental risk. For example, silver recovery processes that use an acid wash create toxic wastes and associated health and safety risks and further contaminate the film, thereby preventing its recyclability.

DuPont established its program to recover silver and polymer from used film largely to address these environmental concerns. DuPont's program is comprised of collection networks, transportation systems, and reclamation centers. Each of these activities is described below and summarized in the figure below.

Collection

DuPont sells its film processing services directly to used film generators, as well as to collectors. DuPont has authorized approximately 350 independent local collectors to pick up and consolidate used film from generators, such as hospitals, clinics, and print shops, and ship the film to DuPont reclamation centers. Thirty-five collectors, however, account for the majority of DuPont's reclamation business. Collection fees are separately

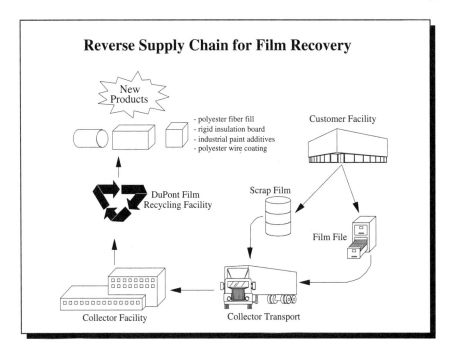

Reverse Supply Chain for Film Recovery

New Products

- polyester fiber fill
- rigid insulation board
- industrial paint additives
- polyester wire coating

Customer Facility

DuPont Film Recycling Facility

Scrap Film

Film File

Collector Facility

Collector Transport

negotiated between generators and authorized collectors selected by the generators.

A typical collector is a small business serving a given area with over 20 years experience in film collection and silver brokerage. In addition to picking up used film, collectors recover silver from solution, sell silver recovery equipment, and service such equipment. These collectors generally have 5,000 to 10,000 square feet of enclosed floor space suitable for sorting used film, packing the film into gaylord boxes (square cardboard boxes that hold about 800 pounds of material), and consolidating outbound freight into truckload quantities. They also typically have two or three panel trucks that are used to pick up used film from local generators.

When DuPont initially established this reverse distribution network, it attempted to enter the market as a retailer. It dealt directly with generators, circumventing local collectors. This tactic, however, proved unsuccessful; using local collectors was a better option. The economics of freight consolidation are important to the business, but the micro-service support that collectors provide to local generators is essential. For example, collectors:

♦ Remove film from shelves, drawers, and storage containers;

♦ Destroy any confidential records and separate and remove extraneous material such as paper folders;

♦ Remove containers from customer premises and consolidate them at their own facilities into trailer load lots (DuPont prefers to receive used film in 800 pound gaylord shipments (3'x3'x3') that are mounted on pallets and loaded 44 to a 48-foot dry van);

♦ Consolidate the film into shipping containers on their premises; and

♦ Properly label the shipments.

DuPont furnishes a material tracking form, which assures the generator that its film has arrived at a DuPont Recycling Facility intact and that the integrity of the shipment will be preserved through the recycling process. Shipment integrity is important, because it relates to both product liability and the value of silver derived from the shipment. In other words, a generator can be held responsible for any liability deriving from its shipment as well as be paid an amount commensurate with the value of the silver in the shipment.

Transportation

Collectors forward used film to one or two DuPont reclamation centers in truckload quantities of labeled containers. Presently, about 75 percent of all shipments that DuPont receives comprise full truckloads of 30,000 to 40,000 pounds each. DuPont offers collectors freight services with pre-arranged and prepaid zone pricing from four regions of the United States to DuPont's two reclamation centers. Freight charges under this program are ultimately absorbed by the collector in the final settlement DuPont makes for the reclaimed silver. Most collectors, however, prefer to arrange their own transportation.

DuPont's reverse distribution chain is paced by the commitments of its two reclamation facilities to produce polyethylene terephalate (PET) plastic raw materials. In essence, it is demand-driven. The flow rate of inbound used film, as well as the production schedule of the two reclamation plants, are designed to support outbound PET commitments.

Scheduling deliveries and making appointments for inbound shipments from collectors and generators is the responsibility of a customer service group in Arden, North Carolina. This center manages the production scheduling system for the entire reverse distribution chain. On average, 5.5 telephone calls are required to plan each inbound load. The customer service group attempts to meter truck arrivals so that they approximately match the facilities' processing capacity: three to four truckloads per day.

DuPont is flexible in its commercial arrangements. It offers generators and collectors a full menu of services. For example, DuPont will either purchase and resell silver reclaimed from generators or simply sell its reclamation services for a fee, leaving the generator with title to the silver until DuPont sells it for the generator's benefit. DuPont will deal with generators either directly or indirectly through collectors of their choice. In both cases, however, freight charges for delivery to DuPont's reclamation centers are absorbed by the shipper. This circumstance makes the consolidation of used film into truckload lots and the intermediation of local collectors essential to preserving competitive economics. Transportation and collection costs are typically three to four cents per pound. By contrast, as noted below, the value of reclaimed polymer is only about five to 30 cents per pound.

Reclamation

The DuPont reclamation centers extract silver and convert the film base into polymer by-products. DuPont uses a proprietary recovery process that avoids air and water pollution, toxic waste, and other environmental problems associated with competing recovery processes. The process extracts silver and creates a clean polyester film base, which can be reused or recycled. Part of DuPont's competitive advantage in this market involves the accuracy of its silver assay technique. The logistical implication of such an assay is that a shipment from each generator must preserve its identity or physical integrity until the assay is completed. If a collector consolidates the used film of several generators, the generators are paid an average price.

DuPont currently operates two reclamation centers that have a combined production capacity of over three million pounds per month. Both facilities operate 24 hours a day, five to seven days per week. One of these centers is located in Arden, North Carolina, near Asheville. It principally serves customers located in the Southeast, as well as DuPont's internal recycling needs. It has 110,000 square feet of enclosed storage capacity for used film. The second reclamation center, which was completed in 1990, is located in Winchester, Kentucky. It serves the Northeast and Midwest markets. It has 80,000 square feet of enclosed storage capacity for used film. More than 65 percent of all used film is generated in these two markets. In addition, DuPont is considering a joint venture with another reclaimer in the West to service the West and Southwest United States and Mexico.

DuPont considers a variety of factors when locating facilities. Proximity to recycled material generators and users of recycled polymers is important. Most of DuPont's polymer customers are located in the Southeast and along the Eastern seaboard. For that reason, the collection and reclamation network has an East Coast orientation. The distance to film generators and recycled polymer purchasers have similar levels of importance because the unit transportation costs are comparable for these materials -- the shipping density of new polymer materials is comparable to that of used film. An additional consideration that has played an important role in locational decisions is facility permitting. In fact, permitting considerations, such as cost, delay, and public relations, can be more important than the total logistics cost of collection and distribution.

Photo Film Value Chain

Two figures below represent the reverse distribution process for photo film. This process involves two distinct reverse distribution paths: one for silver nitrate and one for recycled polymer material.

As shown in the figure on page 241, the reclaimed silver is refined and used as an input in producing silver nitrate, thereby making its way back into film manufacturing. Traditionally, silver recovery involved a set of transactions through which recycled silver moved from generators, to collectors, to reclaimers and refiners, and back into the commodity market as silver nitrate. The source of value in this chain was the spread between the market price of refined silver and the purchase price of recycled materials, minus the costs of handling, transportation, and processing. When silver commodity prices were high ($7.5 per troy ounce) participants in the chain prospered, but when prices were low (currently $3.5 per troy ounce) margins collapsed. Dupont entered this market, not as a commodity trader, but as a seller of reclamation services.

Polymer material (i.e., PET), which accounts for 99 percent of the weight of used film, is either recycled or disposed. (See the figure on page 242.) The recovered polymer base is shipped in truckload lots directly to manufacturing plants, including DuPont plants and third-party facilities. Part of the reclaimed polymer material is thereby returned to the film manufacturing process.

The value of reclaimed polymer typically ranges from about five to 30 cents per pound, depending on the level of contamination. If the contaminated coating is not removed from

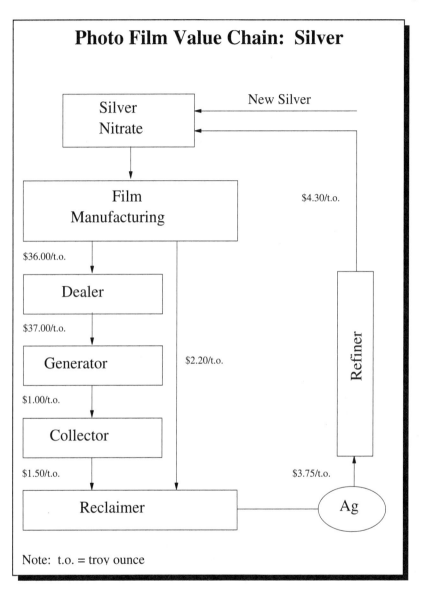

Photo Film Value Chain: Silver

Silver Nitrate

New Silver

Film Manufacturing

$4.30/t.o.

$36.00/t.o.

Dealer

$37.00/t.o.

Generator

$2.20/t.o.

$1.00/t.o.

Collector

Refiner

$1.50/t.o.

$3.75/t.o.

Reclaimer

Ag

Note: t.o. = troy ounce

Photo Film Value Chain: Polymer

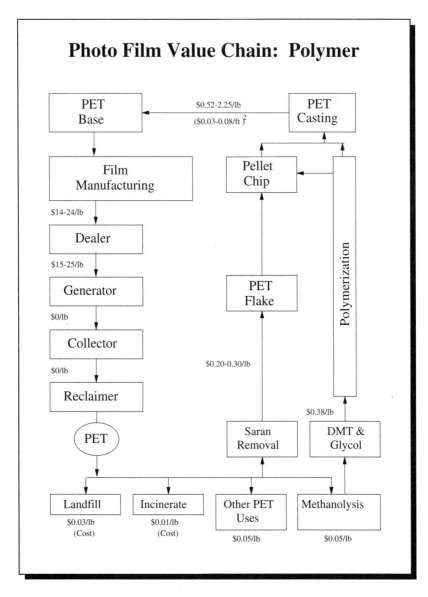

the polymer, the value of the reclaimed material is about five cents per pound. If the coating is removed through the saran removal process, however, the value of the reclaimed polymer increases to 20 to 30 cents per pound. Alternatively, the contamination can be removed through a chemical reversal process known as methanolysis. This process breaks down the polymer into its constituents, dimethyl terephthalate and glycol, which are used in manufacturing film base through the polymerization process. Methanolysis increases the value of recovered polymer to 38 cents per pound, the cost of virgin raw materials. This process requires large capital investments and is energy-intensive.

One of the ways that DuPont attempts to differentiate its services from those of its competitors is cycle time. Cycle time in this system is measured by the elapsed time between the arrival of used film at a DuPont reclamation center and final settlement for silver that DuPont sells for its customers' account. Generators and collectors have a strong preference for accelerated cash flow. DuPont guarantees its customers a 25-day cycle time and measures its own performance against this standard. Currently the average settlement cycle is less than 20 days.

DuPont believes it can create sustainable value in the photo film reverse distribution chain based on the following four assessments:

(1)   Most importantly, it can reuse recycled polymer materials, which competing reclaimers pay to dispose of;

(2)   Its process to assay the silver content of used film materials is more accurate than competing processes;

(3)   Its proprietary process to refine silver reduces the Superfund liability risk to generators and collectors; and

(4)   The collection-to-silver-sale cycle time of DuPont's program is shorter than that of competitors, which accelerates the cash flow to collectors and generators.

DuPont has discovered that the economics at the "back end" of the supply chain are very different from the economics at the "front end." DuPont has also found that attention to logistics detail and continuous refinement of collection, transportation, and reclamation processes is the best way to improve process economics. The challenge of designing recycling systems that produce secondary materials that cost less than virgin materials is difficult.

It has taken DuPont three years and several mis-starts to make the Film Recovery Program viable. Because the field of reverse distribution is still in its incipient stages, there is no one right or wrong way to create a reverse distribution program. DuPont has found, however, that it is important to first achieve market acceptance, and only then to "fine tune" the supply chain. DuPont hopes to soon transfer lessons learned in North America to a reverse distribution chain that it plans to establish in Europe.

8.5 Recycled Photo Chemicals Program

Since launching its Film Recovery Program in 1990, DuPont has progressively added to its product and services line. It now offers two branded photo chemical products, Universal Recycled Fixer and Universal Recycled Developer, which are closely related to film recovery. These products can be reused up to 50 times. The company now takes back and recycles photo fixer and developer, as well as film. While both programs serve the same target markets -- hospitals, clinics, and print shops -- DuPont has developed a distinct supply chain to take back photo chemicals. This reverse distribution chain is described below.

Collection and Transportation

As part of its program, DuPont furnishes waste generators with containers for collecting spent photo chemicals. These containers range in size from five and 20 gallon carboys to 55 gallon drums. Transporting these chemicals is more complicated than transporting used film because spent photo chemicals have been classified by the U.S. EPA as hazardous wastes. Owing to this classification, the chemicals can be transported only in trucks that have hazardous waste hauling permits. A DuPont affiliate that meets this requirement, Conoco Transportation, manages approximately 50 percent of the pickup and delivery within this reverse distribution chain. This arrangement is supplemented by contract carriers where necessary.

Conoco collects and transports carboys and drums of used photo chemicals, including offset printing shops, medical service facilities, and industrial manufacturing plants. The cycle time for the photo chemical reverse distribution chain, measured as the

time between the arrival of the chemicals at a DuPont Processing
Center and the completion of processing, ranges between 15 days
to 30 days. The DuPont customer service group in North
Carolina that manages the flow of used film also manages the
schedule of pickups and the management of truckload flows into
the reclamation centers.

Recycling/Processing

Because used photo chemical transportation costs are high,
accounting for about 50 percent of the cost of recycling photo
chemicals, DuPont Processing Centers for these chemicals are
designed around regional markets that generate large volumes of
spent chemicals. The two existing centers are located in
Lakeland, Florida and East Chicago, Indiana. The Florida
reclamation center caters to markets as far north as Atlanta and
Knoxville, but principally serves Florida. The Indiana center
serves the Midwest. DuPont's next processing center, designed to
serve the Northeast, is planned for the New York State area.
DuPont will develop new regional centers as the photo chemical
recycling market matures.

Photo chemicals arrive at a center in distinct and separate
lots for two reasons: (1) processing is material-specific and (2)
DuPont credits individual customer accounts for the silver
reclaimed from the solutions. This procedure minimizes
opportunities for blending and consolidating chemicals in the
field. Once the chemical "fingerprint" of each separate batch has
been captured at the center, 500 gallon lots are processed.
Presently, the Lakeland facility operates two shifts, five days per
week and the East Chicago facility operates one shift, five days

per week. Eventually, both centers are slated to operate three eight-hour shifts a day, five days a week.

Once the chemicals have been processed, the reclamation plants in Florida and Indiana ship full truckload quantities of the products through DuPont's three regional product distribution centers. Universal Recycled Fixer and Universal Recycled Developer move from these centers through the normal dealer network back to customers.

The Recycled Fixer and Developer Program differs from the Film Recovery Program in several respects, which have necessitated different logistical processes and strategies:

♦ Unlike the film recovery market, which is mature and has well established local collectors, the market for recycled photo chemicals is just beginning to develop as a result of DuPont's initiative. Marketing constraints or limitations on the design of a collection network for this market are therefore less prevalent.

♦ Unlike used film, spent photo chemicals have been classified by the U.S. EPA as hazardous wastes. Hence, their transportation, handling, and storage must comply with strict environmental regulations. All intermediate participants in the supply chain must be licensed to handle hazardous wastes.

♦ The value of photo chemicals per pound is significantly less than the value of used film per pound. Hence, in the case of photo chemicals, tradeoffs between economies of scale in reclamation

and smaller, less transportation-intense local markets
favor shorter transportation hauls and locally-based
reclamation.

♦ The product moving through the photo chemical
reverse distribution chain is liquid while that moving
through the used film supply chain is solid. This
difference has implications for packaging and
handling.

♦ Finally, unlike the open loop film recovery supply
chain, the photo chemicals supply chain is a closed
loop in which generator facilities purchase recycled
fixer and developer from DuPont.

8.6 Reverse Distribution Program Planning Within DuPont

Within DuPont, two planning processes -- one along
technology lines and another along market lines -- intersect and
generate opportunities for value-added reverse distribution
services. The evolution of vertical processes along market lines is
discussed in section 8.2. Along the technology lines, the
corporation maintains a big-picture focus on its proprietary
capabilities to beneficiate complex waste streams. These
capabilities fall generally into the area of molecular engineering.
The continued development of its core competencies in
technology takes place at the corporate level. For example,
DuPont makes strategic decisions through an Environmental
Leadership Council responsible for process leadership in targeted
areas such as polymer waste recovery. The purview of this group
is global and its perspective is long term.

The Council, however, does not focus on the hundreds of specific initiatives and market opportunities that could result from the successful application of DuPont's proprietary technology. This planning responsibility along market lines resides with DuPont's 35 strategic business units. The strategic business units provide the entrepreneurial energy and the market follow-through that apply DuPont's core competencies and assets to specific market opportunities.

Several key drivers present in the current competitive environment affect this planning process:

♦ **Legislative and regulatory developments.** Federal and state environmental laws and regulations are particularly important.

♦ **Customer needs.** DuPont continues to search for new value for customers it already serves through the forward supply chains.

♦ **Continuing societal trends.** DuPont is keenly aware that recycling and reuse have become entrenched in today's culture.

♦ **Perceived value in recovery.** This last point is critical. DuPont applies its technology and resources to new market opportunities only after it determines through supply chain analysis that sustainable value can be created through recycling or reuse.

Once DuPont makes a commitment to a new recycling or reuse service or product initiative, a new supply chain is constructed around the proprietary process and/or product that gives DuPont an advantage in the target market. DuPont has found, after refining its approach to supply chain development, that the distribution network serving the forward supply chain **cannot** be used for reverse distribution. Simply "reversing the flow" does not work for several reasons:

- Interface with waste material generators is complex and requires tailored arrangements, high levels of local service support, and face-to-face interaction.

- The products that DuPont recycles are transportation-intensive with respect to cost. Transport costs account for about 30 percent of product value in collection networks that serve single, national reprocessing centers and about 50 percent of final product value in collection networks that serve multiple regional reprocessing centers. In both cases, consolidation of shipments at a local collection facility is essential to control transport costs.

- A smooth and regular flow of product to the reprocessing or refining centers must be ensured. Most of DuPont's recycling facilities are designed to operate on three eight-hour shifts daily on a five-, six-, or seven-day week. High levels of facility utilization are no less essential than full trailer load shipments in assuring profitable operations.

To support its reverse distribution programs, DuPont assembles service elements within the supply chain (e.g., collection and transportation services and processing facilities), selecting internal capabilities and third-party capabilities based on the following criteria:

♦ **Level of competency.** Does this service element offer best practice capabilities, a strong track record, and genuine management competence?

♦ **Degree of environmental risk or liability.** Is this element of the reverse distribution chain capable of minimizing environmental liability to DuPont by preventing the mismanagement of product waste?

♦ **Cross-functional synergy.** Does DuPont currently use either third-party services or internal services whose capacity utilization could be marginally improved?

♦ **Cost.** Significantly, the last and least critical criterion in this selection process is cost. DuPont believes that best practices and full utilization create the appropriate environment for cost fine-tuning once a supply chain is established.

DuPont has learned that no matter how well-planned a new commercial venture may be, changing customer needs and emerging opportunities lead in unpredictable directions. In particular, DuPont has found that the most effective entry strategy for a new recycling business is to first develop the market, then to analyze the production and logistics economies, and finally to fine tune logistics arrangements and operations. Extensive use of contractors minimizes the risk of initial program startup. Fine tuning the system invariably involves some trial and error.

Creating a reverse distribution program generally requires a collection network, transport systems, and processing facilities. A certain degree of experimentation may be required by way of:

♦ Testing alternative material collection networks through agency or franchising agreements. DuPont has tried both third-party and own account collection. A tradeoff typically exists in this area between third-party collectors' established market relations with local companies and DuPont's desire to sell a collection service differentiated in its quality and professionalism.

♦ Building transport systems that consolidate reused product streams so that they can be returned to DuPont's remanufacturing centers at minimum unit cost. Transport cost is the single largest cost component in DuPont's reverse distribution chains. Over the long run, this cost may also be the most controllable factor that will improve overall logistics efficiency. DuPont minimizes transportation costs by carefully selecting the third-party transportation companies and collectors. The Materials and Logistics division at DuPont often recommends specific trucking services.

♦ Building new facilities to process inbound recycled materials in economic locations. As a precondition, the reclamation process must measure up to best practices and must exceed the most stringent regulatory standards. At the same time, the supply chain organized around the facility must minimize inbound and forward logistics costs. DuPont is successfully pursuing a strategy that involves:

- First winning market acceptance;

- Using third-party contractors to supply reprocessing services during the startup phase; and then

- Building facilities to efficiently support defensible market positions.

Such a strategy minimizes the risk of over-capitalizing this emerging business.

Key Findings

✓ *Reverse distribution is an emerging experimental science. Little derived wisdom and no one right or wrong way yet exists. Hence, innovative experimentation and a flexible, practical response to experiments appears to be the best way to create a viable program at this stage of the discipline's development.*

✓ *Devising a cost-effective transportation system can be essential to ensure the viability of a reverse distribution program. Unit transportation costs at DuPont account for about 30 to 50 percent of product value.*

✓ *Based on DuPont's experience, the best entry strategy for reverse distribution programs is to first achieve market acceptance and then to fine-tune the supply chain. Commitments to establish fixed facilities can be made once the viability of the market has been determined with reasonable confidence. Large capital investments, in any case, are easier to justify based on "cost savings" than on "market potential."*

✓ *Establishing reverse distribution chains to produce recycled materials that are price competitive with virgin materials is not easy. It requires time and substantial management resources to break even. Once the initial market and process commitments have been made, value can be created by fine tuning the process.*

Endnote

1. *Value Line*, May 7, 1993, page 1248.

CASE STUDY: THE HOME DEPOT

9.1 Introduction

The Home Depot, Inc. is one of an established group of "power retailers" that *Business Week* predicts will dominate retail distribution in the 1990s.[1] This select group of giant merchandisers, includes Wal-Mart, K Mart, Toys R Us, Circuit City Stores, Dillard Department Stores, and Target Stores. Power retailers employ the following business strategies:

- Use economies of scale in purchasing and distribution to offer "every day low prices" in their target markets;

- Offer a wide choice of merchandise to their customers; and

- Strive for service excellence by training and motivating their employees.

The enormous buying power of these retailers gives them leverage with vendors when negotiating terms of sale and distribution, and further enables them to influence product design. As Wal-Mart Chief Executive David Glass explained for *Business Week,* "We're probably in a better position to determine specifically what the customer wants than is the manufacturer."[2] The result is a shift in power from manufacturers to retailers.

As a result of their proximity to customers, retailers have been some of the first companies to respond to the growing public enthusiasm for recycling. The debate over environmental correctness has been particularly acute in grocery stores, where clerks now frequently ask customers whether they prefer paper or plastic bags. (The superior bag from an environmental economics standpoint is one the customer must purchase. Consumers, if made to pay the full cost, will tend to purchase reusable (e.g., cloth) bags.) Retailers have also experimented with labeling programs to educate consumers about environmentally friendly products, established collection bins for household recyclables, and developed "green" product lines.

This case study is organized in the following sections:

- ♦ Section 9.2 presents background information on The Home Depot's business;

- ♦ Section 9.3 provides an overview of the firm's waste reduction programs; and

- ♦ Sections 9.4 to 9.6 describe these programs:

  - ‣ Marketing and selling green products;

  - ‣ Recycling in-store waste and product packaging waste; and

  - ‣ Developing buy-back centers for discards from customer construction projects and household recyclables.

9.2 Business Background: The Home Depot

The Home Depot is the largest and fastest growing retailer of home improvement products in the world. The company was founded in 1978 by two former employees of Handy Dan Hardware, Bernard Marcus and Arthur Blank. By 1989, The Home Depot had passed Lowe's Hardware in sales to become the largest retailer of home improvement products in the

Company Statistics (1992)	
Net Sales (billions)	*$7.1*
Number of Stores	*230*
Revenue Per Store	*$633,000*
Products Per Store	*35,000*

United States. In 1992, The Home Depot had sales of $7.1 billion and in recent years the company has achieved annual growth rates of over 20 percent. On average, The Home Depot stores generate $362 per square foot and stock 35,000 items.

Fortune Magazine ranks The Home Depot as one of the 30 largest retailers in the country. Among the power retailers, The Home Depot is unique in its specialized market focus. Its two primary customer segments within this market include do-it-yourself home owners and home improvement contractors. The various categories of merchandise sold at The Home Depot stores are shown in the table below.

The Home Depot's headquarters are located in Atlanta, Georgia. Although the company has 230 stores in 21 states, its strongest presence is in the southern part of the United States, specifically Georgia, Florida, Texas, and California. The company is currently expanding in the Northeast, mid-Atlantic, and Pacific Northwest regions.

The Home Depot Merchandise Mix (1991)

Category	% of Total Sales	Typical Products
Plumbing, heating, and electrical supplies	29%	Rough plumbing supplies, sinks, water heaters, vanities, kitchen cabinets, basic electrical supplies, wiring, light fixtures, kitchen ranges, hoods, bath fans, and decorative ceiling fans
Building materials, lumber, and floor and wall coverings	31%	Dimensional lumber, plywood, particle board, insulation, windows, doors, storm windows and doors, roofing, paneling, vinyl flooring, hardwood floors, shelving, and ceiling tile
Hardware and tools	12%	Hand tools, power tools, nuts and bolts, and other hardware
Seasonal and specialty items	15%	Gardening supplies and tools, plants, lawn mowers, fireplaces, and fireplace equipment
Paint and fixtures	13%	Paint, paint supplies, wallpaper, shutters, and storage shelving

9.3 Overview of Home Depot's Waste Reduction Programs

The Home Depot's management envisions a retail environment that is efficient for shopping as well as stocking and re-supplying. This vision is translated into reality by hiring employees who can provide superior customer service and by devoting careful attention to store design. These principles of The Home Depot's retail strategy also shape its approach to environmental issues. The company's environmental management program is designed to complement its overall growth strategy and to make regulations, like the German Packaging law that would impose mandatory recycling regulations on businesses, unnecessary. Such laws would impose some additional burden on the company, but more importantly, they could theoretically erode the competitive advantage that The Home Depot currently enjoys by virtue of its environmental initiatives.

In The Home Depot organization, waste reduction and related environmental programs are initially developed within the Marketing Department. The Manager of Environmental Marketing, who was hired in 1990, has a strong cross-functional background that includes retail store planning and merchandising experience, as well as industrial engineering experience. He works closely with The Home Depot's Vice President for Traffic and Distribution, the Merchandising Vice President's staff, and the company's Store Operations Vice Presidents to identify, specify, and test new recycling and other waste reduction initiatives.

The organizational environment at The Home Depot is open, informal, and action-oriented. Waste reduction and other environmental initiatives are tested and refined in the field and are quickly dropped if they fail to achieve desired results. To date, The Home Depot has launched the following waste reduction projects:

- Marketing and selling of green products, which includes a partnership with Scientific Certification Systems to verify the environmental claims of products sold in The Home Depot stores;

- Recycling in-store waste and product packaging waste; and

- Entering a joint venture with Mindis Recycling to develop buy-back centers that collect discards from customer construction projects and household recyclables.

Each of these ventures is described in greater detail below.

9.4 Marketing and Selling Green Products

In 1991, The Home Depot formed a working relationship with Scientific Certification Systems, Inc. (SCS), the largest "green" certification organization in the United States. All environmental claims on merchandise sold through The Home Depot are verified by SCS, such as the percentage of recycled content, lack of toxicity, or energy efficiency. Approved products display the SCS Green Cross label and the specific claim. SCS has also developed an "Environmental Report Card" that examines environmental impacts over product life-cycles. (See Chapter 7 for a more detailed discussion of SCS and its Report Cards.) The Home

Depot expects to integrate this approach into its future business efforts.

At present, the retailer is tentatively considering a program to selectively certify the compliance of specific products with a refined eco-code. This eco-labeling system would rely on the SCS label for product environmental attributes and on The Home Depot's own label for products that can be recycled through The Home Depot's affiliated recycling company, described later in section 9.6.

The Home Depot has produced a brochure highlighting the green products available in its stores. Many green products are designed for home use and naturally lend themselves to renovation projects (e.g., low flush toilets, low flow shower heads, water filters, compact fluorescent lights, water-based solvents, insulation, and radon testing kits). The Home Depot integrates these products into its traditional displays, they are not segregated in a special section.

> ### The Environmental Home[3]
>
> *The Home Depot's "Environmental Greenprint*[TM]*" is designed to make homeowners more aware of water and energy conservation, indoor air quality, and other environmental and health threats. "We created the Greenprint to help the customer see the big picture about the many alternative 'green' product choices now available," said Mark Eisen, the firm's Manager of Environmental Marketing.*

The Home Depot has also demonstrated its willingness to discontinue sales of products with apparent negative environmental impacts, if an effective substitute is readily available. In 1991, The Home Depot helped EPA launch a waterborne lead abatement program by becoming the first major retailer to discontinue the sale of lead soldered plumbing products. The Home Depot's research confirmed EPA's assertion that lead solders had a high potential for misuse and the company switched to carrying only products with lead-free solders.

The company also is developing a program to ensure that the wood and wood products it sells are responsibly forested.

9.5 Recycling In-Store Waste and Product Packaging Waste

This section describes three Home Depot waste reduction activities:

(1) Recycling in-store wastes;
(2) Requiring suppliers to take back packaging; and
(3) Reducing or recycling product packaging.

In-Store Waste Recycling

The Home Depot's in-store waste stream consists of corrugated cardboard, wood, pallets, ferrous and non-ferrous metals (including metal straps and bands), plastic materials, computer paper, aluminum cans, and miscellaneous trash. This waste stream comes from three sources: transport dunnage, intermediate packaging, and general office activities.

The Home Depot stores currently recycle 100 percent of their corrugated cardboard and have had programs in place to recover this material since shortly after the first stores opened in 1978. All stores have balers to compact cardboard for economical transportation to local and distant markets. More extensive

Closed Loop Pallet Recycling

The Home Depot's Northeastern region has adopted an innovative closed loop pallet recycling program. Home Depot's stores in this area were being charged $200 to $500 per trailer for collection of old pallets, depending on the end use. To improve its market leverage, the Regional Distribution Manager arranged for backhauling from 12 stores throughout the region to the distribution center and identified two companies that could handle the pallets for less: (1) Nazareth Pallets charges The Home Depot only $60 per 45 foot truck load to collect and repair pallets, but it can handle only limited quantities and (2) Advanced Pallet Recyclers (APR) agreed to charge $200 per trailer to collect, shred, and compost the pallets if Home Depot would sell the pallet compost product in its stores. Most of Home Depot's pallets are currently being composted by APR.

The deal with APR was contingent on its developing a compost product that met Home Depot's standards. First, a team was formed with representatives from distribution and merchandising that worked with the compost company to develop two products: Enviro Mulch 2000 and Root Mulch. The two brands are made by mixing the chipped pallets with different additives. To ensure that the compost did not contain chemicals harmful to plants, samples were evaluated and approved for use by Scientific Certification Systems. The two compost products are sold in bags marked with the SCS green cross seal and in truckload quantities. Home Depot stores purchase the mulch at prices competitive to similar products carried by the stores.

Home Depot does not have a contract to buy a fixed amount of the compost. In the beginning, the Regional Distribution Manager worked actively to ensure that Home Depot stores purchased the pallet compost product, but he is now letting the market take its course. Educating customers, however, increases sales. In stores where clerks explain the origin of the product to customers, demand is high. In one store, the recycled mulch is the only compost product presently offered. APR is now arranging to pick up used pallets directly from some stores where it delivers the compost product, although compost is not delivered as often as the pallets must be collected.

The Home Depot does not regard the composting arrangement as its final solution to the pallet disposal problem. In fact, the company is slowly switching from pallets to slipsheets, which are easier to discard.

recycling programs, such as those that collect customers' plastic nursery containers and recycle Christmas trees, are limited to a few stores, particularly ones in the Atlanta area.

The Home Depot would like to send loads of mixed recyclables comprised of stretch wrap, computer paper, cardboard, aluminum cans, metals, and wood to independently operated materials recovery facilities (MRFs) for processing. Most of the approximately 170 MRFs currently operating in the United States, however, are dedicated to residential recyclables and do not accept mixed commercial wastes. The Home Depot stores do not have sufficient space to store recyclables and do not want to invest employee time in sorting recyclables into categories acceptable to MRFs. The company, however, still manages to send 30 percent of its compactor loads to MRFs.

Packaging Take-Back Initiatives

The Home Depot has begun to include in its competitive supply solicitations the requirement that suppliers take back dunnage, defective supplies, and package waste. The company believes that this tactic can be most effectively used for "commodity" products that lack brand name recognition, since it has greater leverage over vendors of such products. Although the company expects that the added cost of product take-back programs will ultimately be reflected in vendor prices, it believes that its buying power is sufficient to assure that price increases will be spread over its suppliers' entire market bases.

Dunnage take-back is a standard industry practice when suppliers of construction material make direct deliveries at construction sites. The Home Depot believes that its stores should receive the same level of service. So far, The Home Depot has successfully negotiated a take-back arrangement for the space allocators that separate sheets of drywall, thereby saving approximately $700,000 a year in collection and disposal fees based on a $50/ton average collection and disposal cost. An audit of the waste from The Home Depot stores revealed that these spacers accounted for approximately 10 percent of the total in-store waste generated.

Reducing or Recycling Product Packaging Waste

The Home Depot is also looking into ways of reducing product packaging so that consumers have less packaging to dispose of after purchasing products. Reduced packaging would not only help the company achieve its environmental objectives, but would also complement its merchandising system. From the firm's perspective, less packaging implies that more products can be placed on a shelf. In addition, The Home Depot's merchandising strategy -- a "no frills," bulk presentation display format -- reduces the need for excessive packaging. Customers select products from rack storage systems in a manner similar to "warehouse pickers."

Since The Home Depot does not sell its own private label products, it must work with vendors to reduce packaging. The company would like its suppliers to eliminate unnecessary packaging that occupies valuable store space. Achieving packaging reductions, however, is not always easy or feasible since packaging performs two key functions:

(1) **Security.** Packaging is often oversized to make it difficult to remove products unseen from the store,

thereby reducing pilferage. The Home Depot feels that in the near future more sophisticated theft detection systems, similar to those in use at libraries, may eliminate the need for oversized packages for security reasons. For instance, an electronic device that triggers a store alarm could be placed on or built into packages. The alarm would be deactivated at the cash register.

(2) **Protection.** Packaging protects the product from damage, not only during shipment into the store, but "all the way home." Packaging may also protect valuable instructions that are particularly important for hardware items.

The Home Depot is aware that Wal-Mart has experimented with recycling centers adjacent to its retail outlets. After The Home Depot opened its Recycling Depot, Wal-Mart opened its first recycling center in Lawrenceville, Kansas, a 3,000 square foot facility adjacent to its new Eco Store. Kroger and Winn-Dixie have also developed customer recycling centers that are staffed and supported by municipal employees. The Home Depot, however, is reluctant to take back product packaging at the store, in part because the retailer believes that packaging is necessary to protect products on the trip home and because packaging holds operating and assembly instructions. Instead, the company believes that packaging should be carried home and, when recyclable, brought back to a recycling center. Alternatively, the company would consider legislation that makes manufacturers responsible for cradle-to-grave product and packaging management, although the latest experience from the

German system (see section 2.5) makes The Home Depot unlikely to support that approach.

In addition to recycling in-store waste and attempting to reduce and recycle product packaging, The Home Depot is also:

- Replacing pallets with slipsheets made from corrugated cardboard and recycled plastic;

- Purchasing recycled building materials and other environmentally favored products to construct The Home Depot stores whenever possible; and

- Using recycled products for items such as cash register receipts, forms, shopping bags, and store signs.

9.6 Recycling Depot: Reclaiming Customer Waste

This section is divided into three parts. The first part discusses the evolution of the Recycling Depot and the roles played by The Home Depot and its joint venture partner, Mindis Recycling. The second part describes the various stages through which a recyclable product moves after it is dropped off at the Recycling Depot. The third part describes the marketing of secondary materials after processing.

Evolution of the Recycling Depot

The Home Depot's most ambitious recycling project to date is the Recycling Depot, a drop-off center for recyclables adjacent to The Home Depot store in the Atlanta suburb of Duluth, Georgia.

Reuse and Recycling

This project is a joint venture with Mindis Recycling, a U.S. division of London, England-based Attwoods PLC. Mindis Recycling operates a hub and spoke network of 20 scrap buy-back centers organized around approximately 10 processing centers in the Southeastern United States. Together these facilities recovered and processed about 1.3 billion pounds of material in 1992. Attwoods PLC, Mindis Recycling's parent company, is a publicly-held landfill and waste collection firm and is the fourth largest waste services firm in the world.

The Recycling Depot is testimony to the influence of Earth Day 1990 on businesses. Mindis became convinced that its recycling drop-off centers could serve a wider market when customer volumes at existing drop-off sites increased by 400 percent after Earth Day 1990. By Earth Day 1991, Mindis had opened a high profile, Mindis Mart in Marietta, Georgia. It offered customers the opportunity to redeem their recyclables for cash or "environmentally friendly" products in an adjacent retail center. Customers could also choose to donate proceeds to charity.

In the spring of 1992, Mindis decided that a partnership with a major retailer might provide better access to a broader customer base. Mindis approached The Home Depot with the idea of a joint venture and received a favorable hearing. Not coincidentally, the Manager of Environmental Marketing at The Home Depot had participated in the early planning process for the Mindis Mart, which was designed by his former business associate. For The Home Depot, the partnership presented an opportunity to pursue its environmental objectives while reducing its capital investments. Further, The Home Depot stores depend on direct vendor deliveries (i.e., products are not taken to a warehouse before being brought to the stores). This absence of warehouses in the forward supply chain limits the company's ability to collect, consolidate, and reverse distribute customer waste through its own infrastructure.

In February 1993, The Home Depot and Mindis opened the Recycling Depot. This store provides small contractors and homeowners with a convenient alternative to disposing of materials from renovation jobs, such as aluminum window frames, pipes, water heaters, and electrical wires. State and local recycling laws and rising landfill tipping fees are making the disposal of these materials increasingly difficult and expensive. The Recycling Depot also accepts common recyclables such as beverage containers, newsprint, corrugated cardboard, and office paper. As of July 1, 1993, however, the decline in market prices forced the company to charge for these commodities, which effectively suspended their collection.

> **Materials Accepted at the Recycling Depot**
>
> *Water heaters*
> *Stoves*
> *Refrigerators*
> *Metal cans*
> *Electrical wire*
> *Pipes*
> *Other metal products*
> *Beverage containers*
> *PET & HDPE plastic bottles*
> *Glass bottles*
> *Newsprint*
> *Corrugated cardboard*
> *Office paper*
> *Window frames*
>
> *The Recycling Depot does not accept products that contain freon, CFCs, or PCBs.*

The Recycling Depot was designed to expand and improve the Mindis Mart design. With approximately 10,000 square feet of space on a one acre site, the Recycling Depot has the capacity to handle more than one million pounds of material a month. To maximize customer convenience, the Recycling Depot has three lanes for drive-through traffic.

Both the Recycling Depot and Mindis Mart customers receive cash for the items they bring, based on current market prices. While the Recycling Depot does not have retail space for green products inside the drop-off center, a broad range of these products are offered as part of The Home Depot merchandise line.

Both The Home Depot and Mindis wanted to avoid some of the problems experienced by other retailers that have experimented with drop-off centers for recyclables, such as Wal-Mart, Kroger, and Winn-Dixie. These retailers have placed unmanned drop-off containers for plastic bags and other household recyclables inside their stores or in store parking lots. The materials recovered from this type of arrangement have been plagued by high contamination rates. One company that processes used plastic grocery bags complained of receiving everything from cash register receipts to melons and old shoes. The household recyclables collected, other than aluminum cans, have a relatively low value, so the retailers are reluctant to expend staff time to supervise the drop-off boxes or weed out contaminants. In contrast, metal products account for approximately 50 percent of the recyclables received at the Recycling Depot and could help subsidize the collection of household recyclables. Further, to avoid contamination problems, the Recycling Depot's drop-off center is fully staffed.

Under the terms of the partnership, Mindis assumes responsibility for managing the Recycling Depot, which includes setting prices for the recyclables and arranging the marketing and transportation of the recyclables to end-users. The Home Depot rents the land for the facility to the joint venture, advertises the drop-off center in customer mailings, and provides in-house services such as graphic design for signs. Both Mindis and The Home Depot train the Recycling Depot employees so that they are exposed to the culture and operations of both companies. The Home Depot also plans to rotate its store employees through the center, so that they can respond to any inquiries from customers at the retail store about the Recycling Depot's services. The partnership offers both companies the opportunity to sell to each others customers and to expand services for independent contractors, a customer group that both companies want to reach.

Broadening its appeal to small contractors is part of The Home Depot's business strategy. Toward this end, the company continues to expand its selection of merchandise for contractors and has redesigned its store aisles to provide these customers with speedier checkout service. Mindis hopes that the plumbers and electricians who shop at The Home Depot will bring valuable metal scrap, such as copper wire and pipes, to the Recycling Depot.

The partnership with Mindis also provides The Home Depot with an outlet for the recyclables generated by its stores. The Recycling Depot currently receives a variety of materials from the Duluth store and metal products from The Home Depot's other stores in the area. If the partnership is expanded, The Home Depot may have found a solution to the lack of processing facilities for at least some of its commingled commercial waste: it may be able to use the drop-off centers to handle some in-store mixed wastes.

One of the keys to the profitability of manned drop-off centers is balancing staffing levels and store hours with customer service. The Recycling Depot's hours are somewhat shorter than The Home Depot store hours but the Recycling Depot is open much longer than most municipal drop-off centers. The Recycling Depot currently has between two and five employees working shifts during a 66 hour week. To avoid over staffing, employees are trained to perform multiple functions, such as operating the cash register and weighing and sorting materials.

Stages of Recycling

The following paragraphs briefly describe the stages through which recyclable materials move after they have been deposited at the Recycling Depot or any Mindis drop-off center.

Sorting. Once the recyclables are weighed and purchased from customers, the Recycling Depot employees manually sort the material and place it in either compactors or roll-off containers for shipment to processors. Paper and metal products are separated by grade. Glass containers are sorted by color and crushed to make cullet. No special materials handling equipment is needed to move the material from the trucks to the Depot since the products accepted are all small and light enough for customers to have loaded onto their trucks themselves.

Collection and Transportation. The managers at Mindis processing facilities coordinate collection and transportation of materials from Mindis's drop off centers like the Recycling Depot. Sometimes collection routes are combined with pick-ups from large industrial customers. Each processing center has its own driver(s), fleet of semis, roll-off containers, compactors, and tractors. The size of the fleet depends on the volume of material handled at the facility and the distance to markets.

Recyclables are picked up daily from the Recycling Depot and transported either to processing facilities or end-users, depending on the price difference for processed versus unprocessed material (e.g., loose versus baled cans). Paper, plastic, and metal products other than aluminum are usually transported in either roll-off containers or gaylord boxes by truck to Mindis processing facilities in the Atlanta area. Glass and aluminum are usually shipped by truck directly from the Depot to manufacturers, including a Mindis-owned aluminum smelting plant in Tennessee.

Processing. The Mindis processing facilities in Atlanta include facilities include a two million square foot processing center for paper and plastics that used to be a GM factory and several scrap yards that reclaim metal. Specific processing functions include:

- Sorting metal and paper products by grade;

- Shredding steel;

- Cleaning metal, such as cutting iron parts from non-iron products;

- Sorting, cleaning and pelletizing or flaking plastics; and

- Baling or banding products, depending on customer specifications.

After processing, the materials can be stored on site as needed until truckload volumes are reached. Processing facilities, in general, prepare recyclables to be remanufactured into new products and serve as warehouses to store the materials until delivery to customers. Storage at these facilities, however, is a much more informal arrangement than in a warehouse. Instead of being stacked on pallets in rack systems, recycled materials are baled and stacked, kept in roll-off containers, or, in the case of some metals, stored loose in piles.

Material moves in and out of the processing centers daily, but the items are not identified and tracked as they move through the facility. Depending on orders and material type, an item could move in and out in one day although inventories typically turn over each month. (In poor market conditions, inventories may be held until prices rebound, which may take several months.)

The processing facility manager arranges transportation of the recycled materials to the customers designated by the sales staff. Mindis' trucks transport most materials. Contract shippers are used for long hauls or to handle materials overflow. Rail transport may be used depending on cost and customer access to rail lines.

Marketing

With its hub and spoke network, Mindis consolidates the scrap from its decentralized purchasing operations so that the processed recyclables can be sold in high volume shipments. The company's organization reflects this strategy. The sales division is primarily located at the corporate offices in Atlanta, although the company's steel scrap broker is in Birmingham, Alabama.

Mindis has long-term orders for recyclable material with most of its customers and sells just a minimal amount of material on the spot market. Operating with an established customer base simplifies Mindis' marketing efforts. Since most of the materials are shipped to regular customers, arranging transportation is a routine exercise requiring few resources. In contrast, many smaller companies that broker waste or recyclables have to expend time and resources looking for the least cost transportation option to cater to a changing customer base.

Mindis strives to produce the highest quality material possible in order to keep accounts during the periodic downturns in the secondary material markets. Companies that purchase secondary material from Mindis include newsprint deinking plants, steel mills, manufacturers of copper wire, auto parts, glass bottle manufacturers, and companies that make lumber and carpeting from plastic. So far, the Recycling Depot venture has not spawned any new marketing agreements between Mindis and companies that manufacture products for The Home Depot stores. Mindis' customer base, however, does include some of The Home Depot suppliers.

The Home Depot hopes to eventually extend the concept of the Recycling Depot to more of its stores. If a significant number of stores are covered by the program, the company plans to use the Recycling Depot to collect, sort, and recycle products, and perhaps packaging, on behalf of participating vendors who join its collection system. A special label could be placed on the products of such vendors, as noted earlier in Section 9.4. This plan is still in a conceptual stage but it holds interesting possibilities. Indeed, it involves nothing less than closing the supply chain loop.

Key Findings

✓ *Environmental programs that complement a company's other business strategies are more likely than other programs to succeed. At The Home Depot, environmental strategies complement the company's merchandising objectives by providing recycling services to key customer groups and reducing packaging to fit more products on the shelf.*

✓ *Established markets do not always provide solutions for environmental problems. In the case of The Home Depot, the retailer cannot easily recycle in-store waste because MRFs are not geared to handle mixed commercial wastes.*

✓ *The Home Depot's experience illustrates that forging a partnership can enable a firm to achieve its environmental objectives while reducing expenditures for staff or facilities. The Home Depot uses SCS to evaluate green marketing claims for products sold in its stores and its joint venture with Mindis to access a scrap recycling network for in-store and customer waste.*

✓ *The structure of a forward supply chain can influence the difficulty of organizing a reverse supply chain. The Home Depot stores depend on direct vendor deliveries, and the resulting absence of warehouses in the forward supply chain limits the company's ability to collect and consolidate customer waste and its in-store waste through its own infrastructure.*

Endnotes

1. "Clout! More and More Retail Giants Rule the Marketplace," *Business Week*, December 21, 1992, page 68.

2. Ibid, page 66.

3. "The Environmental Home," *In Business*, July/August 1992, page 21.

CONCLUSIONS

10.1 Introduction

Source reduction, recycling, and reuse pose new and interesting challenges to logistics professionals. While the research for this study has found that logisticians have generally not been involved in environmental issues to date, many aspects of waste reduction programs are logistics-intensive and clearly could benefit from the expertise of physical distribution and materials management personnel. The study found that logisticians were most likely to be involved in developing reverse distribution systems for products and packaging, particularly where these systems had the potential to provide companies with competitive advantages in both the economic and environmental arenas.

This chapter outlines the major conclusions that emerged from this study:

♦ Section 10.2 summarizes the factors driving waste reduction programs and reviews the typical three-phase development of corporate recycling and reuse programs.

♦ Section 10.3 outlines the role of logistics in making waste reduction more efficient.

♦ Section 10.4 identifies common themes that emerged from the analysis of logistics problems posed by inbound, forward, and reverse flows of reclaimed materials. This section also serves as a guide to the critical elements of reverse logistics programs.

♦ Section 10.5 highlights the best practices of the companies discussed throughout this book.

♦ Section 10.6 identifies potential next steps that logistics professionals can take to develop reuse, recycling, and other waste reduction programs in their companies.

10.2 The Business Environment

In response to concerns about an apparent landfill capacity crisis and growing public support for environmental initiatives, states have enacted hundreds of waste reduction laws since the mid-1980s. These laws establish recycling and, to a lesser extent, source reduction as the preferred solutions to local solid waste management problems. Comprehensive solid waste legislation is also pending at the federal level. As the costs and difficulties of meeting state mandates for recycling and reducing waste generation have become evident, state and local governments have increasingly looked to manufacturers to shoulder more responsibility for reducing their own wastes and facilitating the recovery of their products.

The threat of additional waste reduction laws coupled with the rising costs of waste disposal are encouraging companies to take a proactive approach to waste reduction. Companies that develop and refine their skills in this area can gain a competitive advantage. Significantly, a number of third-party service providers have stepped forward to offer essential elements of an effective waste reduction program. For example, these companies develop and administer reusable packaging pools, independently verify recycled or green product claims, and offer product take-back and disassembly services.

Waste Reduction Program Development

As discussed in Chapter 3, our research found that corporate waste reduction programs generally follow three phases of development:

(1) Reactive,
(2) Proactive, and
(3) Value-seeking.

These phases correspond with the firm's perception of the potential value of waste reduction activities.

Companies with reactive programs tend to limit their waste reduction activities to regulatory compliance and small scale recycling programs (e.g., office paper and corrugated cardboard). Disruptions to established business practices and new expenditures for waste reduction are kept to a minimum.

Proactive companies are willing to expend more resources on waste reduction initiatives in the belief that such actions may forestall expensive regulations and open up new markets. Proactive companies may expand their recycling programs to include a greater variety of wastes from diverse areas of the firm and create new products and services designed to appeal to the "green" consumers.

Value-seeking companies, meanwhile, have found that commitments to waste reduction can provide strategic advantages. They are willing to commit resources as necessary to develop new business practices. Often, however, they rely on third-party services to reduce their capital investments. These firms may evaluate their products and procedures to identify opportunities to reduce waste internally and to serve the environmental concerns of their customers.

10.3 The Role of Logistics in Waste Reduction

The success of proactive and value-seeking waste reduction programs often hinges on their logistics. Three of the most common activities associated with more advanced programs all involve managing flows of recycled and/or reused materials:

◆ Purchasing recycled material as a manufacturing input;

◆ Reducing, reusing, and recycling wastes from distribution and manufacturing; and

◆ Taking back products and packaging from customers for reuse and recycling,

Purchasing recycled materials from the new municipal recycling programs changes inbound supply chains. Expanding waste reduction programs for internal wastes beyond cardboard and office paper can require establishing new forward distribution systems. Taking back products and packaging from end-users can involve creating reverse distribution systems.

Our research has found that logisticians have generally not been involved with designing or implementing most waste reduction programs, perhaps because the majority of companies that have such programs regard them as compliance tools and/or opportunities to demonstrate good corporate citizenship. Nevertheless, most of the companies interviewed for this study and for other corporate surveys believe that the need for environmental protection is not likely to diminish and that companies must find ways to make recycling and other environmental actions profitable. This paradigm creates an opportunity for logistics professionals to improve the economics of waste reduction programs by making materials reduction, reuse, and recycling activities more efficient.

When waste reduction assumes greater importance within the firm, new career opportunities may arise for logistics personnel. Of the 17 companies interviewed, logisticians played the greatest roles in companies where waste reduction provided significant economic value to the firm, specifically in companies like Xerox, DuPont, Chep USA, and North American Van Lines that have found economic value in taking back their own products and packaging or providing reverse distribution services to others. In fact, some of these reverse distribution systems were established long before environmental issues became important. Most companies, however, are keeping full-time waste reduction staff to a bare minimum. Even proactive and value-seeking companies may leverage small staffs by holding all employees responsible for waste reduction and forming partnerships with other companies.

10.4 Factors Critical to Reverse Logistics Success

Three common themes emerged from our analyses of inbound, forward, and reverse flows of recyclable and reusable material:

(1) The need to improve the efficiency of the collection and processing infrastructure for municipal waste recycling;

(2) The importance of partnerships for implementing waste reduction activities at the corporate level and for building reuse and recycling infrastructures at the industry level; and

(3) The potential for measurement and evaluation systems to track and compare the costs and performance of waste reduction activities.

These issues provide a starting point for companies seeking logistical solutions to waste reduction program design and implementation. Each theme is discussed in more detail below.

Improving the Efficiency of Municipal Solid Waste Recycling

Impediments to the efficient collection, processing, and transport of reclaimed material are similar for inbound, forward, and reverse flows. The differences lie in who is primarily responsible for overcoming the obstacles. Since most recycling markets are demand driven, the collectors and processors of recyclables have traditionally borne most of the responsibility for making recycling efficient. Legislation is now shifting some of the responsibility to product manufacturers and commercial waste generators. Within this community, companies with the most purchasing power are able to set progressive waste reduction policies and shift much of the burden of compliance to their suppliers.

The success of programs aimed at reclaiming products for reuse and recycling is contingent on the factors listed below.

Reducing Market Instability. The newness of the municipal waste recycling infrastructure and product take-back programs creates unstable relationships between secondary materials supply and demand. In closed loop reverse distribution systems, the uncertainty is reduced, but companies still have to match production levels with the recovery of used products.

Resolving Space Shortages. Companies expanding their recycling programs need additional storage space for separated recyclables and processing equipment, such as balers and shredders. Retailers have the most acute space shortages and therefore often need small amounts of material collected frequently.

Balancing Transport Costs and Market Access. The ratio of transportation costs to product value is much higher for recyclable material and used products than for virgin products. Therefore, minimizing transport costs is critical for profitable recycling. In general, the more valuable the recyclable or reusable material, the farther it can be economically transported. Since most packaging materials have relatively low value, finding local markets for them is extremely important. In contrast, more valuable items such as copier machines may be economically transported to regional or national centers for disassembly.

Balancing Processing and Transport Costs. The cost and labor associated with purchasing and operating processing equipment and dedicating storage space must be balanced against the additional revenue generated from the sale of more highly processed materials.

Adopting New Criteria for Siting Plants/Warehouses. Recyclable and reusable materials, as opposed to virgin raw materials, are concentrated in urban areas. To make transportation more efficient, manufacturing facilities that use secondary materials may need to be built closer to cities, and warehouses may need to serve as consolidation and/or sorting points for these materials. Access to rail lines is likely to assume greater importance than in the past, especially for processing facilities, since rail haul can provide significant cost savings over truck transport.

Adopting New Product Design Criteria. Designing for disassembly, such as making parts that snap apart or boxes that collapse after use, can reduce the costs of processing and transporting reclaimed products. Densification processes used for recyclables, such as compaction and shredding, are generally inappropriate for products that must maintain structural integrity for reuse.

Training Employees, Customers, and Carriers. Better communication and training programs are necessary to reduce contamination levels in recyclables collected from in-plant and customer take-back programs. Training programs are also important for introducing service providers to new forms of source-reduced packaging and materials handling techniques that minimize product damage or the need for packaging. These programs also allow the benefits of the waste reduction program to be emphasized.

Partnerships

Companies are entering partnerships to improve the efficiency of the recycling infrastructure, while limiting capital expenditures. Partnerships can range from service contracts, such as DuPont's network of film recovery companies, to strategic alliances that allow both parties to enter new markets, such as The Home Depot and Mindis alliance.

Other benefits of waste reduction partnerships include:

♦ Reducing the uncertainty and quality issues associated with procuring recycled materials;

♦ Improving access to processing facilities and end-markets for in-plant wastes; and

♦ Gaining the expertise and economies of scale needed for take-back programs.

Since reuse and recycling are multi-stage processes that usually involve several different types of companies and often span industries (e.g., glass bottles are remanufactured to make fiberglass and newsprint is used as stuffing in automobile doors), trade associations and industry alliances are playing an important role in making waste reduction more efficient. The companies interviewed for this study have also formed partnerships with other waste generators, companies in the waste management and recycling industries, suppliers, and customers.

Measurement

Corporate waste reduction programs will not be taken seriously unless program performance is measured. Measurement tools include:

♦ **Waste audits** that document the potential supply of waste materials, the percent of such materials being recycled in a company or community, and the relation between waste generation and population or production figures;

♦ **Life-cycle analysis**, which measures the economic and environmental impacts of a product through its manufacture, use, and disposal; and

♦ **Control and information tracking systems** that can link end-users and processors of reclaimed material, allowing them to share information on materials specifications and needed quantities.

Companies generally have been reluctant to take advantage of these tools, believing that the expenditures of time and resources necessary to use them outweigh any potential gains. As waste reduction activities become more important, however, providing quantitative justification for projects and measuring their performance will become increasingly useful. Life-cycle analysis should be a particularly important tool. It can help companies avoid costly investments that have few or negative environmental benefits and identify investments that can create significant long-term savings. Meanwhile, sharing information electronically with other firms in the product reclamation system should become more feasible and desirable as partnerships mature and may bring greater stability to secondary materials markets.

10.5 Best Practices in Reverse Logistics

In interviews with 17 companies and several trade associations, the project team identified specific reverse logistics methods and techniques that, because of their advanced development, deserve to be distinguished as "best." Some of these practices may be transferable to other firms.

Aveda: Striving Toward a Zero Waste Goal

Aveda has a commitment to reuse and recycling that may be unmatched for a company its size. In 1992, the 225-person company diverted more than 85 percent of its waste for reuse and recycling and landfilled just 46 tons of waste from a facility that housed corporate offices, a cafeteria, filling lines, research labs, and the distribution center. Aveda contracts with a recycling company to collect mixed paper and beverage cans. The Environmental Affairs Manager and the Distribution Manager search out vendors for pallets, shipping containers, shrink wrap, packaging peanuts, off-spec product packaging, and food waste and transport low-volume recyclables to markets themselves.

Bristol-Myers Squibb: Information Systems Supporting Take-Backs

Bristol-Myers Squibb Pharmaceutical Group has distinguished itself in developing post-sale product tracking and decision support systems for products returned by customers. This system has evolved from ensuring regulatory compliance to supporting the company's customer relations efforts in a flexible manner. The system tracks products by production lot, expiration date, and chemical composition. It also tracks the commercial parameters that drive the use of the company's product return program.

Chep USA: Pallet Rental and Management Service

Chep USA offers a nationwide pallet rental service to its subscribers. The service eliminates the current pallet exchange program. Distributors are responsible for returning pallets to manufacturers which typically is a burden left to carriers. Chep's third-party managed pallet pool offers benefits to manufacturers, distributors, and carriers. Chep maintains the pallets in good condition, and repositions pallets in response to excess supply or demand. Chep's service organization and computer tracking systems offer participants improved efficiency in product delivery. In addition, the economic life of the pallet has been extended.

DuPont: Applying Internal Solutions to External Markets

DuPont continuously applies its core capabilities in molecular re-engineering to new resource recovery problems. Initially, DuPont developed and refined technologies to reuse materials to solve internal problems and support internal operations. The company subsequently realized that its customers also had unmet needs for material recovery services. Today, DuPont routinely develops recycling and reuse technologies that complement its primary products, refines these technologies internally, and then markets the service to its customers. In this way, DuPont has created several new recycling and reuse markets.

The Home Depot and Mindis: A Strategic Recycling Alliance

The Recycling Depot, a drop-off center for selected construction and demolition debris and household recyclables, is a joint venture between The Home Depot and Mindis Recycling that effectively furthers the marketing strategies of its sponsors. By forging a partnership with Mindis, The Home Depot is able to provide recycling services to a key customer group -- independent contractors -- while also gaining access to a recycling infrastructure for in-store waste. Since the Recycling Depot is sited next to one of The Home Depot stores, Mindis has gained broader visibility for its drop-off centers and a pool of customers that are likely to have valuable metals to recycle.

McDonald's: Testing Waste Reduction Solutions

Even before it announced its widely publicized partnership with the Environmental Defense Fund in 1990, McDonald's Corporation had been searching for ways to reduce and recycle waste from its restaurants. The company is continually testing source reduced packages and has experimented with polystyrene recycling and centralizing contracts for recycling collection services and markets. Currently, McDonald's is expanding corrugated recycling to all of its restaurants, buying more than

Reuse and Recycling

$200 million in recycled products annually, and participating in a national pilot test for composting restaurant waste. Composting has the potential to divert from disposal facilities up to 50 percent of McDonald's restaurants.

Nike: "Bottom up" Recycling and Reuse Programs

Nike's environmental program started from employees' personal concerns about the environment. The company recently launched a recycled content shoe, which originated from the efforts of distribution center employees to divert defective shoes from landfills. The company's full time environmental affairs unit, the Nike Environmental Action Team, grew out of monthly staff meetings of environmentally concerned employees, who took the lead in drafting Nike's 1990 environmental policy statement, identified the need for a formal environmental department, obtained approval from top management, and wrote job descriptions for department members.

North American HVP: Customized Product Take-Back

North American High Value Products (HVP) has developed the essential skills and requisite assets to serve the product reuse and reclamation needs of its customers. The company offers product take-back and de-installation services to manufacturers of electronic equipment, instruments, machine tools, communications equipment, office equipment, and medical equipment. HVP's strength lies in its ability to customize a reuse and recycling network by using as building blocks its trucking fleet, information systems, and international terminal network. Companies benefit from HVP's services in a variety of ways:

♦ They save on administrative, transportation, and information costs;

♦ The value of products recovered for resale is higher when products are properly de-installed and transported; and

♦ HVP helps its customers comply with environmental regulations.

Owens-Brockway: Recycled Content Plastic Packaging

Owens-Brockway was one of the first companies to produce plastic bottles with post-consumer high density polyethylene (HDPE) plastic. The recycled resin is derived from plastic milk bottles collected by residential recycling programs. To produce the new container, Owens had to develop a new manufacturing process and quality control procedures. Owens also changed its inbound transportation network to accommodate small suppliers that are scattered throughout the country, as opposed to the large suppliers of virgin resins that are concentrated in the Gulf Coast.

Procter & Gamble: Leadership in Shaping Public Policy

In the 1980s, Procter & Gamble decided to handle its environmental programs differently from its usual practice of keeping business information close to the vest. The company recognized that by sharing information on its efforts to develop packaging that used less material, contained recycled content, and could be recycled or composted, it could play a leading role in national waste reduction policy development and stay ahead of the legislative curve. The company's strategy has succeeded. Procter & Gamble has won several national awards for its environmental programs and is recognized as having valuable experience to share in policy development forums.

RE-SOURCE AMERICA INC.: Package Recovery System

RE-SOURCE AMERICA INC. offers a patented closed-loop packaging and shipping materials reclamation service designed to reuse resilient packaging 10 to 50 times, thereby keeping packaging material out of the waste stream. The company has worked closely with authorized packaging producers and original equipment manufacturers in creating its recovery system. The system uses specially designed, resilient packaging that can be broken down or compressed for return shipment; provides instructions to end-use customers; and tailors package return services to the specific needs of original equipment manufacturers. Manufacturers benefit from the RE-SOURCE AMERICA INC. system through reduced packaging costs, increased customer loyalty, and an enhanced corporate image.

SCS: Environmental Information Services

Scientific Certification Services (SCS) is pushing the frontiers of green marketing by providing its clients with assessments of the environmental impact of product designs and production and distribution processes. SCS verifies the accuracy of environmental claims made by product manufacturers. It provides customers with multi-faceted yet easily understandable information about the environmental consequences of their choices. SCS has also developed a program to provide procurement managers with environmental information on sourcing options, thereby allowing them to knowledgeably modify procurement specifications.

Sears: Minimizing Shipping Waste

Sears, Roebuck & Co. plans to eliminate 1.5 million tons of shipping packaging annually for products sold at its stores and to recycle much of the remainder to save up to $5 million a year in reduced procurement and disposal costs. Between 1990 and 1992, Sears reduced its cardboard packaging use by 60 percent by arranging for manufacturers to ship apparel in bulk to distribution centers. Previously, about half of Sears' suppliers shipped merchandise in individual cartons directly to retail stores.

Waste Management Inc.: Commercial Recycling Services

Waste Management Inc., the leading provider of curbside collection service for recycling, is now also supplying manufacturers with customized waste reduction services. The company recently constructed a materials recovery facility (MRF) to process waste from an Eastman Chemical manufacturing facility in Tennessee. The Recycle America Tri-City MRF, which is on Eastman property, has served as a catalyst for curbside recycling in local communities. Materials from these programs, which are collected by both Waste Management and municipal crews, are taken to the MRF for sorting.

Xerox: Design of Products for Recycling

Xerox stands out in designing products for remanufacturing. Xerox has designed and built product components since the

1970s whose life span extends in some cases into third and fourth generation use. Xerox uses modular component designs and standard interchangeable parts. The net result is a substantial manufacturing cost savings. The company integrates used components through its new factory configuration that concurrently uses new and used parts to make equipment to the same demanding quality standards. In effect, Xerox has been able to partly substitute highly efficient reverse distribution systems for the procurement of new parts and subassemblies.

Zytec: Reusable Packaging Solutions

Zytec, a Minnesota manufacturer of power supplies for computers, recently switched from cardboard boxes to reusable shipping containers. These containers are sent back immediately unlike the cardboard boxes that had to be stored and disposed of. The new package, which resulted from an employee suggestion, is saving Zytec between $35,000 and $40,000 annually, and conserving storage space at both Zytec and customer facilities.

10.6 Next Steps

The reverse logistics field is evolving so rapidly that most companies undertaking waste reduction programs will be pathfinders. This book describes the reuse, recycling, and other waste reduction practices of some of the first companies to initiate major programs and provides general implementation guidelines based on their experiences. The individual logistics practitioner who wishes to apply this information within his or her company should consider taking the following steps:

♦ Survey the firm's current waste reduction activities;

- Analyze the factors driving the program, such as employee concerns, public attitudes, cost savings, or customer requests;

- Anticipate new developments that could influence program goals, such as pending legislation or scientific findings;

- Develop a plan to increase the efficiency of current waste reduction projects and to initiate new activities that could create both environmental and economic benefits to the company; and

- Work with other departments (e.g., marketing, legal, government affairs, and product design) and top management to refine and implement the plan.

Most importantly, when working on waste reduction projects, expect to continually draw on past logistics experience to find efficient solutions that balance competing corporate goals and incorporate life-cycle costs. Using basic logistics skills will help ensure that these activities provide maximum value to the company.

SOURCES OF FURTHER INFORMATION

This chapter provides a brief listing of publications and organizations that may be helpful to businesses that are considering or implementing waste reduction programs. The references are organized into the following eight categories:

(1) Waste Reduction Guides,
(2) Waste Reduction Laws and Regulations,
(3) Business and the Environment,
(4) Periodicals,
(5) Life-Cycle Analysis,
(6) Recycling Market Information,
(7) Organizations Active in Waste Reduction, and
(8) State and Provincial Recycling Organizations.

11.1 Waste Reduction Guides

These references provide step-by-step guidance or models for business waste reduction programs.

Business Recycling Manual, Inform Inc. and Recourse Systems, Inc., 381 Park Avenue South, New York, NY 10016, (212) 689-4040.

Final Report of the Source Reduction Task Force, Coalition of Northeastern Governors (CONEG), 400 North Capitol NW, Suite 382, Washington, DC 20001.

Bingham, Gail and Christine Ervin, *Getting at the Source: Strategies for Reducing Municipal Solid Waste, The Final*

Reuse and Recycling

Report of the Strategies for Source Reduction Steering Committee, 1991, World Wildlife Fund and The Conservation Foundation, 1250 24th Street, NW, Washington, DC 20037.

Handbook for the Reduction and Recycling of Commercial Waste (1988), Ocean State Cleanup and Recycling, Department of Environmental Management, 83 Park Street, Providence, RI 02903-1037, (401) 277-6012.

The McGraw-Hill Recycling Handbook, McGraw-Hill, 11 West 19th Street, New York, NY 10011.

Recycling Yearbook: A Guide to Recyclable Materials, Case Studies, Organizations, Agencies and Publications, Gale Research, 835 Temobscot Building, Detroit, MI 48226.

11.2 Waste Reduction Laws and Regulations

German Packaging Ordinance: A Practical Guide with Commentary, Institute of Packaging Professionals, 381 Carlisle Drive, Herndon, VA 22070-4823.

Environmental Labeling in OECD Countries, Organization for Economic Co-Operation and Development (OECD), OECD Publication, 2 Rue Andre-Pascal, 75775 Paris, France.

Final Report on Recycled Paper Definitions, Procurement Standards, Measurement Protocol, Labeling Guidelines and Buy-Recycled Initiatives, Recycling Advisory Council (RAC), RAC, 1101 30th Street, NW, Suite 305, Washington, DC 20007, (202) 625-5410.

State Recycling Laws Update, Raymond Communications, 6429 Auburn Avenue, Riverdale, MD 20737-1614, (301) 345-4237.

11.3 Business and the Environment

The following references address environmental issues primarily of concern to businesses.

Blumenfeld, Karen, Ralph Earle III, and Frank Annigbofer, "Environmental Performance and Business Strategy," *Prism*, Fourth Quarter, 1992, pages 65-81.

Cairncross, Frances, *Costing the Earth, The Challenge for Governments, The Opportunities for Business*, Harvard Business School Press, Boston, MA, 1992.

Graham, Ann B., et al., *Managing the Global Environmental Challenge*, prepared and published by Business International and Arthur D. Little, New York, NY, 1992.

Hart, Christopher and Ellen Auster, "Proactive Environmental Management: Avoiding the Toxic Trap," *Sloan Management Review*, Winter 1990, pages 7-18.

Kashmanian, Richard, *Assessing the Environmental Consumer Market*, U.S. EPA, Washington, DC, April 1991.

Monty, Richard, "Beyond Environmental Compliance: Business Strategies for Competitive Advantage," *Environmental Finance*, Spring 1991, pages 3-11.

Reuse and Recycling

Smart, Bruce, Editor, *Beyond Compliance, A New Industry View of The Environment*, World Resources Institute, Washington, DC, April 1992.

11.4 Periodicals

Periodicals listed include those targeted towards professionals in the logistics and waste reduction fields.

Biocycle, Journal of Waste Recycling, Box 351, Emmaus, PA 18049.

Environmental Periodicals Bibliography, International Academy at Santa Barbara, 800 Garden Street, Suite D, Santa Barbara, CA 93103.

Environmental Abstracts, Through EnviroLine, Bowner A&I Publishing, 245 West 17th Street, New York, NY 10011.

Garbage, The Practical Journal for the Environment, 2 Main Street, Gloucester, MA 01930.

Grocery Distribution Magazine, 455 South Frontage Rd., #116, Burr Ridge, IL 60521.

Green Market Alert, 345 Woodcreek Road, Bethlehem, CT 06751, (203) 266-7209.

Green Marketplace, The Bridge Group, 345 Wood Creek Road, Bethlehem, CT 06751.

The Logistics Environmental Analysis Framework (LEAF), A directory to information resources on logistics and the environment. Contact Dr. Helferich, Director, Materials and Logistics Management Program, The Eli Broad College of Business, Michigan State University, East Lansing, MI 48824-1121, (517) 355-2177.

Materials Handling Engineering, 1100 Superior Avenue, Cleveland, OH 44114.

Recycling Today, 4012 Bridge Avenue, Cleveland, OH 44113, (216) 961-4130.

Resource Recycling,[1] 1206 NW 21st, Portland, OR 97209.

Traffic Management, Cahners Publishing Co., 275 Washington Street, Newton, MA 02158-1630.

Transportation & Distribution, 1000 Superior Avenue, Cleveland, OH 44114.

Waste Age, 1730 Rhode Island Avenue, NW, Suite 1000, Washington, DC 20036.

11.5 Life-Cycle Analysis

The following references were chosen to provide the reader with a general understanding of life-cycle analysis. The last three sources contain the <u>results</u> of life-cycle analysis.

Bailey, Paul E., "Life-Cycle Costing and Pollution Prevention," *Pollution Prevention Review*, Winter 1990-91, pages 27-39.

Reuse and Recycling

Bailey, Paul E., "Full Cost Accounting for Life Cycle Costs: A Guide for Engineers and Financial Analysts," *Environmental Finance*, Spring 1991, pages 13-29.

Blanchard, Benjamin S., *Logistics Engineering and Management*, Fourth Edition, NJ, Prentice Hall, Englewood Cliffs, 1992.

Brown, R.J. and R.R. Yanuck, *Introduction to Life Cycle Costing*, AEE Energy Books, Atlanta, GA, 1985.

Dhillon, B.S., *Life Cycle Costing: Techniques, Models, and Applications*, New York, NY, Gordon and Breach, Science Publishers, Inc., 1989.

Fabrycky, W.J. and B.S. Blanchard, *Life Cycle Cost and Economic Analysis*, Englewood Cliffs, NJ, Prentice Hall, 1991.

Kirkpatrick, Neil, *Selecting a Waste Management Option Using a Life-Cycle Analysis Approach*, PIRA International, Randalls Road, Leatherhead, Surrey KT22 7RU, UK, tel (code UK + 44) 0372 376161; fax (code UK + 44) 0372 377526.

The Tellus Packaging Study, May 1992, Tellus Institute, 89 Broad Street, Boston MA, 02110, (617) 266-5400. (Available in a 50 page summary or a 900 page complete report.)

The Environmental Packaging Yearbook, Published by Packaging Strategies/Green2000, 122 South Church Street, West Chester, PA 19382, 1-800-524-PACK.

11.6 Recycling Market Information

American Recycling Market Directory/Reference Manual, Recoup Publishing Limited, P.O. Box 577, Ogdensburg, NY 13699, (800) 267-0707.

Fibre Market News, 156 Fifth Avenue, New York, NY 10010. (Contains broker and dealer prices for a wide variety of textile and paper grades.)

Official Board Markets, 111 East Wacker Drive, 16th Floor, Chicago, IL 60601. (Publishes paper mill prices primarily for paperboard and corrugated cardboard.)

Recycling Times, 1730 Rhode Island Avenue, NW, Suite 1000, Washington, DC 20004. (Publishes end-user and dealer price information for a variety of MSW recyclables.)

The following is a listing of state or regional waste exchanges.

Alabama Waste Materials Exchange
Linda Quinn
404 Wilson Dam Avenue
Sheffield, AL 35660
(205) 383-5630

Alberta Waste Materials Exchange
Cindy Jensen
Building #350
6815 8th Street, N.E.
Calgary, AB T2E 7H7
(403) 297-7505
Fax (403) 297-4548

Arizona Waste Exchange
Barrie Herr
4725 E. Sunrise Drive
Suite 215
Tucson, AZ 85718
(602) 299-7716
Fax (602) 299-7716

Arkansas Industrial Development Council
Ed Davis
#1 Capitol Hill
Little Rock, AR 72201
(501) 682-1370

B.A.R.T.E.R.
Jamie Anderson
2512 Delaware Street, S.E.
Minneapolis, MN 55414
(612) 627-6811

British Columbia Waste Exchange
Jill Gillette
102 1525 W. 8th Avenue
Vancouver, BC V6J 1T5
(604) 731-7222
Fax (604) 734-7223

Bourse Quebecoise des Matieres Secondaires
Dr. Francois Lafor
14 Place Du Commerce,
Bureau 350
Le-Des-Squeurs, PQ H3E 1T5
(514) 762-9012
Fax (514) 873-6542

California Waste Exchange
Claudia Moore
P.O. Box 806
Sacramento, CA 95812-0806
(916) 322-4742
Fax (916) 327-4494
(Hazardous Waste)

CALMAX
Joyce Mason
909 12th Street, Suite 205
Sacramento, CA 95826
(916) 255-2369
Fax (916) 255-2221
(Solid Waste)

Canadian Chemical Exchange
Philipe La Roche
P.O. Box 1135
Ste-Adele, AB JOR 1LO
(800) 561-6511
Fax (514) 229-5344

Canadian Waste Materials Exchange
Robert Laughlin
2395 Speakman Drive
Mississauga, ON L5K 1B3
(416) 822-4111
Fax (416) 823-1446

Hawaii Materials Exchange
Jeff Stark
P.O. Box 1048
Paia, HI 96779
(808) 579-9109
Fax (808) 579-9109

Hudson Valley Materials Exchange
Jill Grouper
P.O. Box 550, 1 Veterans Drive
New Paltz, NY 12561
(914) 255-3749
Fax (914) 255-4084

IMEX
Bill Lawrence
506 2nd Avenue, Room 201
Seattle, WA 98104-2311
(206) 296-4899
Fax (206) 296-3997

Indiana Waste Exchange
Jim Britt
P.O. Box 454
Carmel, IN 46032
(317) 574-6505
Fax (317) 844-8765

Industrial Materials Exchange Service
Diane Shockey
P.O. Box 19276
Springfield, IL 62794-9276
(217) 782-0450
Fax (217) 782-9142

Intercontinental Waste Exchange
Anne Sternberg
5200 Town Center Circle, Suite 303
Boca Raton, FL 33486
(800) 541-0400
Fax (407) 393-6164

Iowa Waste Reduction Center
By-product and Waste
Search Service
Susan Salterberg
75 BRC–University of
Northern Iowa
Cedar Falls, IA 50614-0185
(319) 273-2079
Fax (319) 273-2893

Kentucky Department of Environmental Protection
Charles Peters
18 Riley Road
Frankfort, KY 40601
(502) 564-6761

Louisiana/Gulf Coast Exchange
Rita Czek
1419 CEBA
Baton Route, LA 70803
(504) 388-4594
Fax (504) 388-4945

Manitoba Waste Exchange
Todd Lohvinenko
1812-330 Portage Avenue
Winnipeg, MB R3C 0C4
(204) 942-7781
Fax (204) 942-4207

Minnesota Technical Assistance Program
Helen Addy
1313 5th Street, Suite 307
Minneapolis, MN 55414
(612) 627-4555

Missouri Environmental Improvement Authority
Thomas Welch
325 Jefferson Street
Jefferson City, MO 65101
(314) 751-4919

MISSTAP
Caroline Hill
P.O. Drawer CN
Mississippi State, MS 39762
(601) 325-8454
Fax (601) 325-2482

Montana Industrial Waste Exchange
Montana Chamber of
Commerce
P.O. Box 1730
Helena, MT 59624
(406) 442-2405

New Hampshire Waste Exchange
Emily Hess
122 N. Main Street
Concord, NH 03301
(603) 224-5388

New Mexico Materials Exchange
Four Corners Recycling
Dwight Long
P.O. Box 904
Farmington, NM 87499
(505) 325-2157
Fax (505) 326-0015

Northeast Industrial Waste Exchange
Carrie Maus-Pugh
620 Erie Boulevard West
Suite 211
Syracuse, NY 13204
(315) 422-6572
Fax (315) 422-4005

Oklahoma Waste Exchange Program
Fenton Rude
P.O. Box 53551
Oklahoma City, OK 73152
(405) 271-5338

Olmsted County Materials Exchange
Jack Stansfield
Olmsted County Public Works
2122 Campus Drive, S.E.
Rochester, MN 55904
(507) 285-8231
Fax (507) 287-2320

Ontario Waste Exchange
Mary Jane Henley
2395 Speakman Drive
Mississauga, ON L5K 1B3
(416) 822-4111
Fax (416) 823-1446

Pacific Materials Exchange
Bob Smee
1522 N. Washington Street
Suite 202
Spokane, WA 99201-2454
(509) 325-0551
Fax (509) 325-2086

Portland Chemical Consortium
Dr. Bruce Brown
P.O. Box 751
Portland, OR 97207-0751
(503) 725-3811
Fax (503) 725-3811

RENEW
Hope Castillo
P.O. Box 13087
Austin, TX 78711-3087
(512) 463-7773
Fax (512) 475-4599

ReSource Exchange Services
Brendan Prebo/
Howard Hampton
213 East Saint Joseph
Lansing, MI 48933
(517) 371-7171
Fax (517) 485-4488

Rocky Mountain Materials Exchange
John Wright
1445 Market Street
Denver, CO 80202
(303) 692-3009
Fax (303) 534-3200

SEMREX
Anne Morse
171 W. 3rd Street
Winona, MN 55987
(507) 457-6460

South Carolina Waste Exchange
Doug Woodson
155 Wilton Hill Road
Columbia, SC 29212
(803) 755-3325
Fax (803) 755-3833

Southeast Waste Exchange
Maxie May
Urban Institute UNCC
Charlotte, NC 28223
Fax (704) 547-3178

Southern Waste Exchange
Eugene B. Jones
P.O. Box 960
Tallahassee, FL 32302
(800) 441-7949
Fax (904) 574-6704

Vermont Business Materials Exchange
Connie Leach Bisso
P.O. Box 630
Montpelier, VT 05601
(802) 223-3441
Fax (802) 223-2345

Wisconsin Bureau of Solid
Waste Management
Lynn Persson
P.O. Box 7921
Madison, WI 53707
(608) 267-3763

11.7 Organizations Active in Waste Reduction

Organizations selected for this list produce written materials
or provide services of particular use to businesses that are
implementing waste reduction programs. To order a complete list
of trade associations, government agencies, environmental groups
and professional societies that are active in waste reduction,
contact the *Resource Recovery Report*, (202) 362-6034.

American Paper Institute
260 Madison Avenue
New York, NY 10016
(212) 340-0600

American Plastics Council
1275 K Street, N.W.
Suite 500
Washington, DC 20006
(202) 371-5679

Coalition for
Environmentally
Responsible Economies
(CERES)
711 Atlantic Avenue
Boston, MA 02111
(617) 451-0927

The Composting Council
114 South Pitt Street
Alexandria, VA 22314
(703) 739-2401

Glass Packaging Institute
1801 K Street, N.W.
Suite 11051
Washington, DC 20006
(202) 887-4850

**Institute of Scrap
Recycling Industries**
1627 K Street, N.W.
Suite 700
Washington, DC 20006
(202) 466-4050

**Institute of Packaging
Professionals**
481 Carlisle Drive
Herndon, VA 22070-4823
(703)-318-8970

**Management Institute for
Environment and Business**
1220 Sixteenth Street, N.W.
Washington, DC 20036
(202) 833-6228

**National Association for
Environmental
Management**
1440 New York Avenue, N.W.
Washington, DC 20005
(202) 966-0019

**National Electronic
Manufacturers Association**
2101 L Street, N.W.
Washington, DC 20037
(202) 457-8400

**National Oil Recyclers
Association**
12429 Cedar Road
Suite 26
Cleveland Heights, OH
44106
(216) 791-7316

**National Polystyrene
Recycling Company**
c/o **New England CRINC**
4 Kildeer Court
Bridgeport, NJ 08014
(609) 467-9044

**National Recycling
Coalition**
1101 30th Street, N.W.
Suite 305
Washington, DC 20006
(202) 625-6406

National Solid Wastes Management Association
1730 Rhode Island Avenue, N.W.
Suite 1000
Washington, DC 20036
(202) 659-4613

National Softdrink Association
1101 16th Street, N.W.
Washington, DC 20005
(202) 463-6732[2]

National Tire Dealers and Retreaders Association
1250 I Street, N.W.
Suite 400
Washington, DC 20005
(202) 789-2300

National Wooden Pallet and Container Association
1625 Massachusetts Avenue, N.W.
Suite 200
Washington, DC 20036
(202) 667-3670

The Portable Rechargeable Battery Association
1000 Parkwood Circle
Suite 430
Atlanta, GA 30339
(404) 612-8826

Solid Waste Composting Council
601 Pennsylvania Avenue, N.W.
Suite 900
Washington, DC 20004
(202) 638-0182

U.S. Army Logistics Management College
Fort Lee, VA 23802-6044
(804) 765-5000

11.8 State and Provincial Recycling Organizations[3]

The following organizations may be useful to businesses that are implementing waste reduction programs, providing specific information on local considerations. Where available, addresses and phone numbers are listed for each organization.

Alabama Recycling Coalition
P.O. Box 241373
Montgomery, AL
36124-1373
(205) 277-0032

Arizona Recycling Coalition
101 S. Central Avenue
Phoenix, AZ 85004

Arkansas Recycling Coalition
P.O. Box 190825
Little Rock, AR 72219-0825

California Resource Recovery Association
4395 Gold Trail Way
Loomis, CA 95650
(916) 652-4450

Rocky Mountain Recyclers Association, (Colorado)
P.O. Box 224
Denver, CO 80214
(303) 441-9445

Connecticut Recyclers Coalition
P.O. Box 4038
Old Lyme, CT 06371
(203) 434-2501
Fax (203) 779-2056

Recycle Florida Today Inc.
P.O. Box 32906
Palm Beach Gardens, FL 33420

Georgia Recycling Association
2980 Cobb Parkway
Suite 192-100
Atlanta, GA 30339
(404) 974-4334

Recycling Association of Hawaii
162B North King Street
Honolulu, HI 96817
(808) 599-1976

Illinois Recycling Association
407 S. Dearborn
Suite 1775
Chicago, IL 60605
(312) 939-2203
Fax (312) 939-2536

Indiana Recycling Coalition
P.O. Box 20444
Indianapolis, IN 46220-0444
(317) 283-6226

Iowa Recycling Association
2742 E. Market Street
Des Moines, IA 50317

Kentucky Recycling Association
4837 Madison Pike
Independence, KY 41051

Maine Resource Recovery Association
c/o **Maine Municipal Association**
Community Drive
Augusta, ME 04330
(207) 942-6772

Maryland Recyclers Coalition
P.O. Box 6097
Annapolis, MD 21401
(410) 553-2082

MassRecycle
75 Day Street
Fitchburg, MA 01420
(508) 345-6918

Michigan Recycling Coalition
P.O. Box 10240
Lansing, MI 48901
(517) 371-7073
Fax (517) 485-4488

Recycling Association of Minnesota
(612) 482-1143

Missouri Recycling Association
P.O. Box 1093
Jefferson City, MO 65102
(314) 634-3731

Associated Recyclers of Montana
P.O. Box 1549
Great Falls, MT 59403
(406) 252-5721

Nebraska State Recycling Association
1615 Howard Street
Suite 283
Omaha, NE 68102
(402) 444-4188

Nevada Recycling Coalition
(702) 829-6872

New Hampshire Resource Recovery Association
P.O. Box 721
Concord, NH 03302
(603) 224-6996

Association of New Jersey Recyclers
(908) 722-7575

New York State Association for Reduction, Reuse and Recycling
(315) 685-3874

North Carolina Recycling Association
7330 Chapel Hill Road
Suite 207
Raleigh, NC 27607
(919) 851-8444

Association of Ohio Recyclers
P.O. Box 67202
Cuyahogh Falls, OH 44222
(216) 867-0493

Association of Oregon Recyclers
P.O. Box 15279
Portland, OR 97215
(503) 255-5087

Pennsylvania Resources Council
P.O. Box 88
25 W. Third Street
Media, PA 19063
(215) 565-9131

South Carolina Recycling Association
P.O. Box 7464
Columbia, SC 29202
(803) 252-9250

Recycling Coalition of South Dakota
P.O. Box 84041
Sioux Falls, SD 57118-4041
(605) 333-2341

Tennessee Recycling Coalition
P.O. Box 23796
Nashville, TN 37202

Recycling Coalition of Texas
P.O. Box 2359
Austin, TX 78768

Association of Vermont Recyclers
P.O. Box 1244
Montepelier, VT 05601
(802) 229-1833

Virginia Recycling Association
2735 Hartland Road
Falls Church, VA 22043
(703) 203-0680

Washington State Recycling Association
203 E. Fourth Avenue
Suite 422
Olympia, WA 98501
(206) 352-8737

Associated Recyclers of Wisconsin
16940 W. Shadow Drive
New Berlin, WI 53151
(414) 679-2132

Wyoming Recycling Association
c/o **DEQ-SWHP**
122 West 25th
Cheyenne, WY 82002

Reuse and Recycling

<u>Canada</u>

**Recycling Council of
Alberta**
4646 Builders Road, S.E.
Calgary, AB T2G 4C6
(403) 287-1477

**Recycling Council of
British Columbia**
3102 1525 W. Eighth
Avenue
Suite 102
Vancouver, BC V6J 1T5
(604) 731-7222

**Recycling Council of
Manitoba**
1812 330 Portage Avenue
Winnepeg, MB R3C 0C4
(204) 942-7781

**Recycling Council of
Ontario**
489 College Street
Suite 504
Toronto, ON M6G 1A5
(416) 960-1025

**Saskatchewan Waste
Reduction Council**
101219 22nd Street, East
Saskatoon, SK S7K 0G4
(306) 931-3242

Endnotes

1. *Resource Recycling* also publishes several supplemental updates for specific materials, including *Bottle/Can Recycling Update* and *Plastics Recycling Update.*

2. The National Softdrink Association is a source of information on Beverage Industry Recycling Programs (BIRPs). BIRPs are independently-run recycling programs funded by industry in various states to promote recycling. Three successful state programs are Florida BIRP (407) 678-4200, Missouri BIRP (314) 636-2487, and Kansas BIRP (913) 273-6808.

3. "State and Provincial Recycling Associations Mature," *Resource Recycling*, May 1993, page 35.

GLOSSARY

Baler is a machine used to compress recyclables into bundles to reduce their volume. Balers are often used on newspaper, plastics, and corrugated cardboard.

Composting is the controlled biological decomposition of organic solid waste under aerobic conditions. Composting is a type of recycling.

Construction and demolition debris is waste generated by the construction, remodeling, repair, or demolition of buildings, bridges, pavements, and other structures.

Hazardous waste is waste material that may pose a threat to human health or the environment, the disposal and handling of which is regulated under Subtitle C of the federal Resource Conservation and Recovery Act (RCRA).

HDPE (high-density polyethylene) is a type of plastic used in making containers for milk, juice, liquid detergents, bleach, cosmetics, and medicines.

LDPE (low-density polyethylene) is a type of plastic used in trash bags, diaper backing, and self-serve grocery bags.

Logistics is the process of planning, implementing, and controlling the efficient, effective flow and storage of goods, services, and related information from point of origin to point of consumption for the purpose of conforming to customer requirements. Note that this definition includes inbound, outbound, internal and external movements, and return of materials for environmental purposes.

Materials recovery facility (MRF) is a centralized facility that sorts and processes mixed solid wastes into new products available for market. This term is often use interchangeably with intermediate processing center (IPC).

Municipal solid waste (MSW) is post-consumer non-hazardous solid waste generated by households, commercial establishments, institutions, and light industry. MSW generally excludes construction and demolition debris, most scrap metal, and non-hazardous materials derived from manufacturing processes.

PET (polyethylene terephalate) is a type of plastic used in making such containers as carbonated soft drink bottles and peanut butter jars.

Post-consumer wastes are materials or products that have served their intended use and have been discarded after passing through the hands of a final residential or commercial user. The term excludes materials from industrial processes, such as manufacturing scrap.

Primary packaging is the packaging that comes into direct contact with the product.

RCRA is the Resource Conservation and Recovery Act, a federal law that regulates the management of hazardous wastes (Subtitle C), non-hazardous solid wastes (Subtitle D), underground storage tanks (Subtitle I), and medical wastes

(Subtitle J). It also establishes procurement guidelines requiring federal agencies to purchase recycled materials (Subtitle F).

Recyclables are materials that, after serving their original purpose, still have useful physical or chemical properties and therefore can be recycled into new products.

Recycling is the process by which materials otherwise destined for disposal are collected, processed, and remanufactured into new products. Composting is a form of recycling.

Reuse is the use of a product or component part in its same form for the same use without remanufacturing. Reuse may be considered as a form of source reduction.

Reverse distribution is the process by which a company collects its used, damaged, or outdated products and/or packaging from end-users. Reverse distribution is a subset of reverse logistics.

Reverse logistics is a broad term referring to the logistics management skills and activities involved in reducing, managing, and disposing of hazardous or non-hazardous waste from packaging and products. It includes reverse distribution, as defined above, which causes goods and information to flow in the opposite direction of normal logistics activities. This book focuses narrowly on the non-hazardous waste reduction activities of the reverse logistics process.

Secondary material is recycled material that is used in place of primary or virgin material in manufacturing a product.

Secondary packaging is wrapping around the primary packaging or wrapping that joins together two or more primary packages for consumer sale (e.g., a six-pack ring).

Source reduction entails reducing the amount and/or toxicity of materials destined to enter the waste stream.

Superfund is the common name for the federal Comprehensive Environmental Response, Compensation, and Liability Act (CERCLA), which addresses the cleanup of abandoned or inactive sites contaminated with hazardous substances.

Tertiary packaging is shipping boxes or other packaging materials for product transport (e.g., master cartons).

Tipping fees are the charges, usually in dollars per ton, levied for the unloading or dumping of waste at a landfill, MRF, or other waste management facility.

Waste exchange is a computer and catalog network that helps redirect waste materials back into manufacturing or reuse processes by matching companies generating specific wastes with companies that use those wastes as manufacturing inputs.

Waste reduction is a broad term that encompasses recycling, reuse, and source reduction.